Making the
Early Years Foundation Stage
work for you
(30–60+ months)

by

Dr Hannah Mortimer

Acknowledgements
Based on the approach devised by Helen M. Rowlands
The children, staff and head teacher of Brompton Community
Primary School EYFS Unit
Illustrations by Robyn Gallow
Cover photographs from Busy Bees Childcare
Excerpts from *The Early Years Foundations Stage* (DCFS, 2008)

A QEd Publication

Published in 2008

© Dr Hannah Mortimer

ISBN 978 1 898873 59 4

British Library Cataloguing
A catalogue record for this book is available from the British Library.

Published by QEd Publications, 39 Weeping Cross, Stafford ST17 0DG
Tel: 01785 620364
Website: www.qed.uk.com
Email: orders@qed.uk.com

Printed by Gutenberg Press, Malta.

Contents

Introduction

The Early Years Foundation Stage (DCFS, 2008) provides support and guidance for those working with children aged between birth and 60+ months. This manual is intended to be used in conjunction with the framework for children aged 3 to 5+ years and offers practical hints, tips and sample activities to help give you a real head start.

In this introductory section a number of sample activities have been prepared to help individuals or groups get to grips with using this manual. These exercises will provide valuable training sessions in understanding how the framework really works and how to plan meaningful activities for the children in your care. The exercises have been tried and tested in many nursery settings and we feel confident that because of their very simplicity staff will find them invaluable.

Throughout the section the ☞ symbol has been used to indicate a practical activity. Tick the box on the right when you have completed it to help you keep track of your progress.

Putting the manual into practice

Take some time to look through the manual and you will find that the core principles are the same throughout each section. There are sample activity sheets illustrating ways of applying each individual Focus of Development. At the end of each section there are blank activity sheets. In this introductory section you will be shown how to complete your own activity sheets and slot them into your planning. This means that there is no need for you to read slavishly through the entire manual, simply select the Area of Learning that you will be working with and focus on applying the framework to a child in that group. Once you are confident that you understand the implications with regards to that one child, transfer the framework to others in the age group. Once you have done this, and identified the differences inherent in the group, you should then look further and apply the same principles to another child from a different age group, or in a different Area of Learning. In this way you will find that everything slots into place very comfortably.

In order to simplify the use of gender, we have alternated fairly loosely between male and female throughout the manual.

Because it is usual that practitioners work alongside one or two others closely, as well as additional practitioners in neighbouring age groups, we suggest that introducing this method at a training session with your team will have the most beneficial effect. We have continued in this section with a suggested outline for your workshop, but of course you may choose to follow this in isolation until you feel comfortable enough to continue.

Where to start?

As you are aware, the EYFS framework is separated into six **Areas of Learning**:

- Personal, Social and Emotional Development
- Communication, Language and Literacy
- Problem Solving, Reasoning and Numeracy
- Knowledge and Understanding of the World
- Physical Development
- Creative Development

This manual covers the typical age range of 30 to 60+ months. The first book in this series focuses on 0 to 36 months.

The EYFS is subdivided into typical (though flexible) age bands:

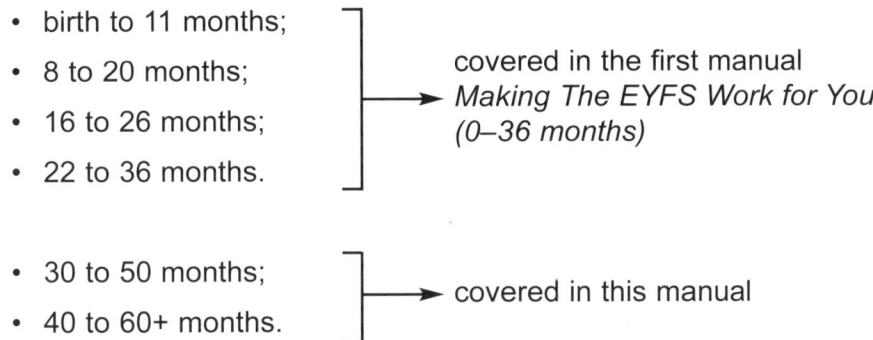

- birth to 11 months;
- 8 to 20 months;
- 16 to 26 months;
- 22 to 36 months.

covered in the first manual
Making The EYFS Work for You (0–36 months)

- 30 to 50 months;
- 40 to 60+ months.

covered in this manual

Each Area of Learning is subdivided into various focuses of Development Matters (we abbreviate this throughout as Focus of Development) and these are listed at the start of each section, together with a simple coding system shown on page 15.

To ensure that our record-keeping and planning can be as simple as possible, this simple code has been allocated to each of the Areas of Learning and Focus of Development throughout the framework.

	Activity	Tick when completed
☞	In the manual, key areas of each of the Focuses of Development are listed so take a little while now to familiarise yourself with the pages referring to Personal, Social and Emotional Development. There is no need at this point to go over the Sample Activity pages. Copy page 15 for ease of use.	
☞	Once you have done this, photocopy pages 6 and 7.	
☞	Gather together a pencil or crayon in each of six colours – purple, pink, green, blue, red and light brown. Collect a yellow highlighter too. Read 'A morning in the life of Jack Morris' and using your purple crayon lightly colour over the parts of Jack's morning that you feel reflect his Personal, Social and Emotional Development.	

A day in the life of Jack Morris, aged 3 years and 3 months

Time	Activity	Focus
9:00	Jack arrives with his nan, and comes straight into the nursery. His nan steadies him and helps to remove his jacket. He hangs it on his peg with the picture of the elephant and puts his flask on the table. His nan draws him back for a quick 'goodbye' but he rushes towards the other children, eager to start the day.	
9:05	Jack notices that the computer is free and he sits on the small bench in front of it. He is soon joined by Shani and the two watch the screen for the story of 'Little Red Riding Hood', clicking the mouse to turn the 'pages'. After the story ends, he tells Liz, one of the adults, that he has had his turn now and leaves the bench to join a group of children at the sand tray.	
9:15	Jack enjoys a game with Sol, pouring sand over each other's hands. As Sol builds mounds up, Jack smoothes and flattens the sand with his spade. He continues to fill different containers, smoothing them over when they are full, with deep concentration.	
9:25	Jack has left the sand tray and has joined a game outside. A pirate area has been created by a group of children who are marching quickly up and down the yard chanting 'we have gold!'. A net has been stretched across one corner and a woven sculpture activity has been adapted into the pirates' hoard as they capture their treasure and poke it through the mesh. Jack finds some paper, screws it up and tries to push it into the mesh, working out how to manage this.	
9:35	Jack goes inside to find the trolley. He pulls it outside, carefully negotiating the doorway and the other children, and joins Tamara who is playing with a pile of wooden bricks and planks. They start to fill the trolley with bricks, holding each high and announcing what each 'is' as it tumbles into the trolley – 'A tiger!' he calls. Tamara pulls the trolley as he steadies the load. One of the wooden shapes is a large cone. He tries to fit this into his pocket and finds he has to turn it pointed-end-down in order to poke it in.	
9:45	The pirates have turned a den into a prison and arranged bins and boards around to enclose their space. There is some negotiation between them about who can come in and who cannot. Jack, one of the younger children in the group, is initially denied. He tries to play with a piece of string but finds that a pirate has the other end of it. After a brief upset, Liz intervenes and helps them to sort out an arrangement together. Jack goes on to collect more string and lengths of wool and, together, the pirates build a web across their door.	
10:00	Jack moves back to the computer where he engages with an early number programme. He is joined by an audience of three other children and they all count out loud as each image comes up on the screen. When the computer voice asks, 'What number comes after eight?', the others chant 'Nine!' and Jack watches, listens and echoes. He clicks the mouse appropriately and announces, 'I'm India Jones!'	
10:05	Jack is attracted back to the pirate area. His friend has come to tell him that the robbers have run away with their money and they need more money to buy candy to give them more power to catch more robbers. Jack comes to help. They have to climb over, under and through various obstacles as they seek for more treasure. They make walkways from low planks balanced onto blocks.	
10:10	Jack moves into the making area. He sits and draws, gathering his sheets of paper into a pile ready to take to his nan. He selects many different sizes, colours and shapes of paper and experiments with different coloured pens and crayons.	

Time	Activity	Focus
10:15	Snack time is flexible and Jack wanders into the cookery area and selects a baby cucumber which he eyes rather suspiciously, tastes and then abandons. He enjoys a tomato and talks with an adult and a few of his friends as they eat.	
10:20	Yesterday, the group had visited a sculpture park and the photographs have already been mounted on card and bound together with treasury tags. Jack sits on the floor with some other children as they look through the photographs and talk about who and what they can see. They recall memories of their trip and talk with their teacher about what they enjoyed most. Their teacher helps them put each photograph into context and think about what each sculpture reminded them of. She helps them develop ideas for their own models and sculptures.	
10:25	The same photographs and more have been loaded into the computer and the children continue to enjoy watching and talking about pictures of their visit. As they crane to see the images, Liz suggests that Jack needs to sit down as his feet are going into Sam's space. He sits where they can all see, leaping up whenever he catches sight of himself or his nan. One picture is of Jack on a miniature train looking brave and this gives the teacher the opportunity to talk about feelings.	
10:35	Jack moves to a writing area and wipes the whiteboard clean. He grasps the pens with a fisted grasp and enjoys making large circular movements and mark-making within the enclosed spaces that he has created.	
10:40	Jack is at a table of dough. He selects a cutter and makes indentations into his ball of dough. He searches for other resources and begins to cut and mould shapes to fit a patty-pan tray. He works out that he needs to flatten his balls of dough in order to make impressions with the cutters.	
10:45	Jack is helped to put his jacket on and he moves outside into the larger of two yards to play. He hangs and swings from the climbing frame. He spots that a tricycle has become available and makes a dash for it. There is a brief skirmish as Jack and another child negotiate whose turn it is and one of the older children steps in to help. Jack then briefly becomes one of many goal keepers in a game of football. Another skirmish results in Jack accidentally pushing another child who falls and hurts his nose. Liz steps in to help and Jack's teacher talks to him about what happened. Jack goes indoors to sit quietly with her for a while.	
10:55	Jack is intrigued by a model helicopter and examines it carefully, turning its blades with his fingers and opening the doors. He moves on to the construction area and begins to make his own miniature sculpture - it looks like a cross between a helicopter and a flying bug, based on some of the sculptures that he had seen yesterday. He adds more pipe cleaners and then concludes, 'My's a e'fant!' ('Mine's an elephant!').	
11:05	It is tidy-up time. Jack joins in a little with encouragement and is thanked for helping.	
11:15	Jack helps his teacher choose the story. They choose his favourite and he sits quietly in the group, enthralled by the story and the pictures. Sometimes he joins in with the familiar catchphrases as the teacher pauses for the children to join in. For a little while, he is distracted by a board game on a nearby shelf, but soon leaves this to follow the story again.	
11:25	The parents and carers have arrived. He remembers his pictures and collects them to show proudly to his nan who is waiting outside the door. She helps him with his coat, reminds him to fetch his flask and he is off home.	

What next?

You may find that you have coloured in quite a lot of text, but don't worry. Because the framework encompasses many of the ordinary but vital parts of a child's development it is natural that there will be some overlap.

Some of these examples might help you check that you are on the right track:

- At 10.25 Jack is looking at photographs of the group's trip to the sculpture park on the computer. He is helped to sit where they can all see, and leaps up whenever he catches sight of himself or his nan. This shows us clearly that Jack can demonstrate that he has developed a sense of personal identity. This is part of his 'Self-confidence and Self-esteem' within his Personal, Social and Emotional Development.

- At 10.45 Jack is helped to negotiate whose turn it is on the tricycle and one of the older children steps in to help. After another skirmish, Jack's teacher talks to him about what has happened. This is all going to help Jack work as part of a group or class, taking turns and sharing fairly, understanding that there need to be agreed values and codes of behaviour for groups of people, including adults and children, to work together harmoniously. You will recognise this as one of the Early Learning Goals within the focus of 'Making Relationships', again within the Area of Personal, Social and Emotional Development. Though Jack has not achieved this goal just yet, there are several examples that he is beginning to learn about turn-taking and sharing such as at 09.05 when he announces that his turn on the computer is over and at 09.45 when he learns to share the string with the other pirates and to cooperate on using it together to form a web.

Once you are comfortable with your inclusions for 'Personal, Social and Emotional Development', move on to the other five Areas of Learning and Development, using a different coloured crayon each time.

	Activity	Tick when completed
☞	This time, read through and find the time slots that typify each of the other five Area of Learning and Development.	

Take another look at 'A morning in the life of Jack Morris'. Can you see areas that overlap? If you can, this means that you are seeing the wider picture and looking at Jack's learning and development as a whole. This, of course, is just what we should seek to do.

Sample activity pages

Take a look at the first sample activity page (page 19) in the Personal, Social and Emotional Development section. This will help you use the activity pages in isolation (from the manual and the EYFS framework) and ensure that you have *all* of the key information to hand on just one piece of paper. You will recognise these headings:

- Area of Learning title.
- Focus of Development title.
- Age range.
- Development matters.
- Play and practical support.
- Note.

What you will not be familiar with are the elements relating to the activity itself:

- Sample activity.
- What you need.
- How to prepare.
- What to do.
- Things to say.
- Comments.

The sample activity is a means of reminding ourselves about the type of activity that might address the issues identified in the Area of Learning pages. They also serve as a really good reminder for those times when we feel that we need a little refresher when drawing up our plans.

In order to guide your session, as much information as possible has been included while at the same time keeping it manageable. There is a list of what you need, even when these resources might appear obvious to the experienced teacher or practitioner. There is detailed information about how to prepare and what to do. Of course, you can be a lot more specific when drawing up your own plans, listing your own equipment in your specific location. The idea in all of these activities is that they should act as a springboard for your own ideas and be used flexibly to suit your particular situation and the children's individual needs. There are also suggestions for things to say - not just questions to ask but commentaries to add or suggestions which open up new options. You can add your comments about how the activity went or how you would like to develop the children's learning in the future in the box at the bottom of each activity page.

In line with the EYFS framework, there is a section which makes suggestions for what you might 'note' – taken from the 'look, listen and note' columns of the Learning and Development grids. The notes that you make will serve as prompts for adding to each child's individual record.

Drawing up your own activity planner

If you are working through this section as part of a team meeting or staff training event, you might like to split into groups for the next activity. It is recommended that you all choose the same activity to draw up though, as this will serve to highlight the differences, and, of course, the importance of noting down exactly what you had intended from the very beginning.

	Activity	Tick when completed
☞	At the back of each section you will find a blank activity planner (pages 36, 59, 75, 98, 112 and 128). Start by photocopying these for you to practise on.	
☞	Because we need to make a start somewhere, go to your planner for next week and choose the activity scheduled for Monday morning.	
☞	Starting with the 'Sample activity' row, take your time and complete the form up to and including the 'Things to say' row.	
☞	Once completed, take a good look at the activity you have drawn up and then spend some time thinking about where this activity would best fit into the EYFS framework. When you are happy with this, move on to complete the 'Area of Learning' title.	
☞	Look at it further before completing the Focus of Development title – you will find you need to turn through the pages of the EYFS Learning and Development Grids to help you decide.	
☞	Once you have done this turn to the 'Development Matters' pages at the start of each section that outline the Development Matters focuses in more detail. Enter the wording just as it appears in the EYFS Learning and Development grids. Remember that your activity planners may be used in isolation from the actual EYFS guidance so you need to have all the important wording with you on the sheet.	
☞	Before you enter the 'Play and practical support' section on your activity planner, consider any amendments that you might like to make to suit your particular situation. Do this now.	
☞	Finally, look once more at your completed activity planner. Would your activity benefit from additional notes in the 'Comments' section?	
☞	If you have split into several groups for this activity you should feed back to each other now. It is important that everybody is comfortable with what you have done so far before moving on to the next activity.	

Hopefully you can now see why we started with this activity. Being able to use your observations (as in 'A morning in the life of Jack Morris') is one skill, but it is also important to use our forward planning to ensure that every focus and Area of Learning and Development is covered for every child. Let us take some time now to practise this forward planning.

	Activity	Tick when completed
☞	Return to the same groups, but this time select different Areas to plan for. If you have six groups you could suggest that you select activities as follows:	
	Group 1 ⟶ Personal, Social and Emotional Development	
	Group 2 ⟶ Communication, Language and Literacy	
	Group 3 ⟶ Problem Solving, Reasoning and Numeracy	
	Group 4 ⟶ Knowledge and Understanding of the World	
	Group 5 ⟶ Physical Development	
	Group 6 ⟶ Creative Development	
	This time start by completing the activity planner from the top down, referring to the Development Matters pages at the start of each section (or using the EYFS Learning and Development grids) for confirmation of the requirements of the activity.	
☞	Now feed back to each other. Remember that each group needs to *inform* the others about exactly how and why the activity meets the requirements of the Areas of Learning.	

Remember at this stage to remind everyone to be open to questioning. We all need to be comfortable that we understand what we are doing before we move on to the next section. Take some time to see each of the activities planned with a child in mind from that age group. Does it fit? Are there alterations to be made now that you can see a specific child doing the activity? Are there alterations to be made if you give the planner to a particular practitioner? Will your descriptions need to be clearer or do you need to specify health and safety issues? Remember to ask yourself these kinds of questions regularly as you plan for your setting.

There is one more exercise before we can discuss fitting our activity planners into our schedule. Think about an activity such as sand play. Of course, playing in the sand involves 'Designing and Making' . . . or is it 'Exploring Media and Materials'? Perhaps it involves 'Shape, Space and Measures' or 'Self-confidence and Self-esteem'. Well actually it can be all of these things and more besides. The key here is to identify clearly the Focus of Development that you are planning for and make sure that your planner is completed accordingly.

	Activity	Tick when completed
☞	For the final exercise in this section return to the same groups and select a different Area and focus of learning completely at random. Ask the group to plan a sand activity that fits. Take only five minutes for this exercise as it is the realisation that we can do this that is the point, rather than the plans themselves that matter.	

Although sometimes we might identify just one small aspect of play that is relevant, we can make sand play fit into *any* of the Areas of Learning and Development. Imagine how useful this is for a child who is only comfortable at one or two rather narrow activities and needs support to become more comfortable in different situations in the future – you immediately have a 'starting point' for working within the EYFS with that child.

Using the framework to support your team

Looking closely at our 'Morning in the life of Jack Morris', you will see how often the unplanned parts of Jack's session can be included when assessing his development. We saw focuses of development being covered as he arrived at the beginning of the session and left at the end of it. Snack times and outdoor play times covered more. Although we remember that all these times 'count', how often do we forget to record them?

	Activity	Tick when completed
☞	Take some time to look through Jack's session again and highlight with a yellow highlighter those unplanned events that can be recorded in Jack's Tracker (or developmental progress chart).	

By doing this you will have drawn up a list of activities or events that are covered by the EYFS framework but that need no, or very little, planning on your part. You will, of course, need to remember to record them and remind all practitioners that these events are important too. Every now and again when you see a Focus of Development being covered spontaneously, note down the appropriate code with the child's name on a Post-it note. Stick this on a grid for later recording.

Once this is completed you will then have a long list of Focuses that are not likely to be covered unless you include them in your plans. This will probably include art and craft activities, music, story times and physical challenges among others.

Take another look at your planner for next week. Part of it might look a little like this (though yours will have many more activities planned per session):

Monday	Tuesday	Wednesday	Thursday	Friday
Visiting day	Feeling good	Mirror box	Magic carpet	Collecting friends
I spy, you spy	Gone fishing	Give me a 'b'!	Tea for two	My home
Anything you can do	Artistic me	On the ball	Conveyer belt	Taking the lead

It certainly looks very interesting. In order to make this a more purposeful planner, what we need are some developmental focuses. Each of these sample activities appear later in the book and these are the Focuses of Development that we have decided to use them for:

Monday	Tuesday	Wednesday	Thursday	Friday
Visiting day **PSED 1**	Feeling good **CLL 1**	Mirror box **PSED 2**	Magic carpet **CLL 2**	Collecting friends **PSED 3**
I spy, you spy **CLL 3**	Gone fishing **CLL 4**	Give me a 'b'! **CLL 6**	Tea for two **PSRN 2**	My home **KUW 5**
Anything you can do **PD 1**	Artistic me **CD 1**	On the ball **PD 3**	Conveyer belt **CD 2**	Taking the lead **CD 3**

You will find a list of the codes used on page 15.

So we have planned for the following Focuses of Development:

PSED 1	Dispositions and Attitudes
PSED 2	Self-confidence and Self-esteem
PSED 3	Making Relationships
CLL 1	Language for Communication
CLL 2	Language for Thinking
CLL 3	Linking Sounds and Letters
CLL 4	Reading
CLL 6	Handwriting
PSRN 2	Calculating
KUW 5	Place
PD 1	Movement and Space
PD 3	Health and Bodily Awareness
CD 1	Being Creative – Responding to Experiences, Expressing and Communicating Ideas
CD 2	Exploring Media and Materials
CD 3	Creating Music and Dance

You will know the abilities of your groups and will be familiar with the Trackers* (or development progress charts) for each of the children you work with. You will therefore be able to use your planning to reinforce areas from these Focuses of Development where support is needed. Later in the year, a similar activity might be planned with reinforcement and encouragement at a later stage of development.

Using the activity planners for the first time

Look again at your activity planner for next week. You probably have several core activities planned per session. When you begin to use the planning system in this book, take things gradually. You will have already made some activities up as part of your group discussions so, if you feel happy with them, start by planning to include these. Try to have at least two activities written up on planners each day. It will take a few weeks to cover all the Areas of Learning but, over this time, you will also be recording spontaneous events. As you become more confident in using the system and build up a bank of sample activities you will be able to demonstrate your detailed plans to any visiting inspector and the recording of spontaneous activity as well!

*The Trackers referred to here are those published by QEd Publications (contact details at the front of the book). *Trackers 0–5: Tracking children's progress through the Early Years Foundation Stage is a* simple and effective way of monitoring progress.

Monitoring your progress

Let us look once more at Jack Morris. We have built up a picture of him as making progress across all six Areas of Learning and Development. Yet he is only three. How can we ensure that he continues to develop into a confident and competent young being? For Jack, it will be important that we monitor his progress closely over a period of time and build up a picture of any Area that he may not, for whatever reason, be accessing. Pay special attention to any gaps and to any particular strengths and weaknesses. Imagine, for example that Jack was doing so well that he really needed more challenge and extension to prevent his becoming bored and frustrated. All we need to do is to look at the next 'Development Matters' entries in the EYFS Learning and Development grids and plan for him to move on. There is no need to be bound by the age restriction. The ages are there simply because in most cases they are appropriate. In some they are not. Remember that this can work both ways and it may be helpful to dip into earlier 'Development Matters' stages in order to provide more support or to meet a child's special educational needs.

Over a period of a few weeks you will be able to see a picture developing of some familiar Focuses of Development reoccurring regularly throughout your planners. What you might not spot so easily are any Focuses being regularly overlooked. You will need to develop your own system for helping you spot these, but one of the most efficient ways is to use a regular 'A morning in the life of . . .' observation for each of the children in your group, as demonstrated in Jack Morris. If you take more detailed notes on one or two children each session, you will be able to analyse these for 'curriculum cover' and they would also make personalised records to share with and delight parents and carers. There are examples of how to use your observations to analyse cover in the last pages of this book, both for a three year-old and a four-year old over their EYFS session.

Summary

By the time you have completed all of the exercises in this book and worked with the system for a month or so you will be able to:

- identify and plan for each of the 30 to 50 month and 40 to 60+ month age ranges in the *EYFS* framework;

- draw up specific activity planners to guide and support the practitioners in your setting;

- make additional comments each time the activity is carried out to keep other practitioners informed;

- record spontaneous events in a similar format;

- evaluate your planning;

- further identify gaps to be addressed in your children's development by transferring observations made to developmental Trackers*.

And finally

To make this manual a *real* success for your EYFS team it will be important to remember that this should be a working document. Make comments about questions raised, lessons learned or even nightmare activities that should *never* be repeated unless we take a number of precautions first.

Summary of codes used

Personal, Social and Emotional Development
PSED 1   Dispositions and Attitudes
PSED 2   Self-confidence and Self-Esteem
PSED 3   Making Relationships
PSED 4   Behaviour and Self-Control
PSED 5   Self-care
PSED 6   Sense of Community

Communication, language and Literacy
CLL 1   Language for Communication
CLL 2   Language for Thinking
CLL 3   Linking Sounds and Letters
CLL 4   Reading
CLL 5   Writing
CLL 6   Handwriting

Problem Solving, Reasoning and Numeracy
PSRN 1   Numbers as Labels and for Counting
PSRN 2   Calculating
PSRN 3   Shape, Space and Measures

Knowledge and Understanding of the World
KUW 1   Exploration and Investigation
KUW 2   Designing and Making
KUW 3   ICT
KUW 4   Time
KUW 5   Place
KUW 6   Communities

Physical Development
PD 1   Movement and Space
PD 2   Health and Bodily Awareness
PD 3   Using Equipment and Materials

Creative Development
CD 1   Being Creative – Responding to Experiences, Expressing and Communicating Ideas
CD 2   Exploring Media and Materials
CD 3   Creating Music and Dance
CD 4   Developing Imagination and Imaginative Play

Personal, Social and Emotional Development

(30–60+ months)

Personal, Social and Emotional Development
(30–60+ months)

Section index

Sample Activities

		30 – 50 months	40 – 60+ months
PSED 1	Dispositions and Attitudes	Page 19	Page 20
PSED 2	Self-confidence and Self-esteem	Page 22	Page 23
PSED 3	Making Relationships	Page 25	Page 26
PSED 4	Behaviour and Self-Control	Page 28	Page 29
PSED 5	Self-care	Page 31	Page 32
PSED 6	Sense of Community	Page 34	Page 35

A blank planner for you to copy and complete for the children is on page 36. There are also non-specific blank planners for you to copy and complete at the back of the book.
There is a monitoring sheet for you to use and adapt on page 37.

Code: PSED 1

Personal, Social and Emotional Development

Dispositions and Attitudes

Development Matters

30 – 50 months
- Seek and delight in new experiences.
- Have a positive approach to activities and events.
- Show confidence in linking up with others for support and guidance.
- Show increasing independence in selecting and carrying out activities.

40 – 60+ months
- Display high levels of involvement in activities.
- Persist for extended periods of time at an activity of their own choosing.
- **Continue to be interested, excited and motivated to learn.**
- **Be confident to try new activities, initiate ideas and speak in a familiar group.**
- **Maintain attention, concentrate, and sit quietly when appropriate.**

You will find suggestions for *Look, listen and note*, *Effective practice* and *Planning and resourcing* in the EYFS Practice Guidance.

Personal, Social and Emotional Development

Personal, Social and Emotional Development
Dispositions and Attitudes (30 – 50 months)

Development matters	Play and practical support
Show increasing independence in selecting and carrying out activities.	Look for opportunities to allow choice and selection in most of your activities. Talk to each child early in the session to help them plan ahead what they would like to do that day, and ask them how it went later.

Sample activity	**Visiting Day**
What you need	A large bear or soft toy and a digital camera.
How to prepare	Simply have out your usual range of EYFS activities and resources.
What to do	At the beginning of the session, introduce Bear and explain that he or she has come to visit the group for the day. Ask for a group of children to look after Bear and show him round. If necessary, help groups of children take it in turns. Ask them to call you whenever Bear is trying out a new activity so that you can take a photograph. If necessary, make suggestions of what Bear might like to see or do next. Later, compile your photographs and ask the children for commentary to write in beneath as a record of Bear's First Day at Nursery. This record would make a wonderful child-centred prospectus which you can use to welcome next terms' children into the group. Parents and carers might be given copies to talk through with the new starters.
Note	Note how ready the children are to try out a range of activities. A spider's web tracking observation can be used to record where they took Bear (as in the example alongside, taken from *The Observation and Assessment of Children in the Early Years*).
Things to say	• What did Bear enjoy doing most? • Has Bear tried the construction toys yet? • Also, take time deciding on the words the children would like to use to describe the photographs you took.
Comments	

Personal, Social and Emotional Development

Personal, Social and Emotional Development
Dispositions and Attitudes (40 – 60+ months)

Development matters	Play and practical support
Be confident to try new activities, initiate ideas and speak in a familiar group.	Using ICT makes it so easy to record your experiences and outings in a way that can be easily shared between the children. Use it to print off photographs or produce a slide show for the computer.

Sample activity	Thanks for the Memory
What you need	Digital camera, computer, (and someone experienced in using ICT!)
How to prepare	When you have had a particularly enjoyable experience or been on a special trip together, take a series of photographs. This activity works especially well if they include whole families sharing fun together – parents, carers, siblings. Make sure that each and every child features frequently in your photographs. Enter them into the computer as a slide show which the children can easily operate.
What to do	While the memory of the outing or special activity is still fresh in everyone's minds, encourage the children to gather round the computer and watch the slideshow. Shy children are usually encouraged to call out or point to themselves as they see each new photograph and the inclusion of other family members in the photographs usually raises confidences to speak. You can also print off and laminate a selection of photographs and connect them with treasury tags for easy page-turning and sharing. Once the children become more confident to speak, share the slideshow on a screen or interactive whiteboard within the whole group.
Note	Observe how confident each child is to join in with this activity and whether they are willing to speak yet in front of the group. Note samples of what they say and their reactions to the photographs.
Things to say	• Can you see yourself? • Where's . . .? • What was happening there? • What happened next?
Comments	

Personal, Social and Emotional Development

Personal, Social and Emotional Development

Self-confidence and Self-esteem

Development Matters

30 – 50 months
- Show increasing confidence in new situations.
- Talk freely about their home and community.
- Take pleasure in gaining more complex skills.
- Have a sense of personal identity.

40 – 60+ months
- Express needs and feelings in appropriate ways.
- Have an awareness and pride in self as having own identity and abilities.
- **Respond to significant experiences, showing a range of feelings when appropriate.**
- **Have a developing awareness of their own needs, views and feelings of others.**
- **Have a developing respect for their own cultures and beliefs and those of other people.**

You will find suggestions for *Look, listen and note, Effective practice* and *Planning and resourcing* in the EYFS Practice Guidance.

Personal, Social and Emotional Development

Personal, Social and Emotional Development
Self-confidence and Self-esteem (30 – 50 months)

Development matters	Play and practical support
Have a sense of personal identity.	Circle times make good starting points for talking confidently – keep the group small and familiar to begin with.

Sample activity	Mirror Box
What you need	A special little box or casket and a small mirror that fits the bottom of its inside.
How to prepare	Glue the mirror firmly to the bottom of the inside.
What to do	During circle time, introduce the little box and tell the children that there is something rather special inside. They can each take a peep but try not to tell anyone else what they can see there! Encourage them to take it in turns as they pass the closed box to each other and then open it to peek inside. Support anyone who is not sure by allowing them to 'pass' or supporting them as they look inside individually either before or after the activity with the group. The first time round the circle, simply look and see. The second time, encourage the children to talk about what they can each see. You can use the box for many circle time activities, such as a simple sentence-completion game: 'I like my . . .' or 'I think I look like . . .' or 'My eyes are . . .' (etc.)
Note	Observe how confident each child is to talk about themselves.
Things to say	• What can you see? I told you it was rather special . . . • I think that it is special because (find affirming things to say about each child).
Comments	

Personal, Social and Emotional Development

Personal, Social and Emotional Development
Self-confidence and Self-esteem (40 – 60+ months)

Code: PSED 2

Development matters	Play and practical support
Respond to significant experiences, showing a range of feelings when appropriate.	Your usual range of soft toys can adopt many personae and can be used in various flexible ways. This activity uses them to engender sympathy and caring in the children.

Sample activity	Poor Bears!
What you need	A selection of soft toy bears or equivalent – visit your local charity shop perhaps (and wash all the bears first). You also need plenty of warm, dry towels, cushions and bedding.
How to prepare	The night before, wet each soft toy and place it in a plastic bag in your freezer. Whilst still frozen, remove the bears from their bags and hide them around your outdoor play area.
What to do	Simply wait for this activity to unroll! Before long, one of the children will have discovered a frozen bear and probably drawn your attention to it. Gather the children around and talk about what you can all do to help poor Bear. The children might want to warm Bear with a cover or dry Bear off in the sunshine or in towels. Before long, several frozen bears will have emerged and will need looking after. This activity leads beautifully into some theme work on hibernation or weather.
Note	Observe the range of feelings that children display and how they make these known. Note examples of what the children say and do when faced with the frozen bears.
Things to say	• Oh dear . . . poor Bear! How can we make Bear feel better? • What happens when you are cold? • I wonder what the Bears were doing?
Comments	

Personal, Social and Emotional Development

Code: PSED 3

Personal,
Social and
Emotional
Development

Making
Relationships

Development Matters

30 – 50 months
- Feel safe and secure, and show a sense of trust.
- Form friendships with other children.
- Demonstrate flexibility and adapt their behaviour to different events, social situations and changes in routine.

40 – 60+ months
- Value and contribute to own well-being and self-control.
- **Form good relationships with adults and peers.**
- **Work as part of a group or class, taking turns and sharing fairly, understanding that there needs to be agreed values and codes of behaviour for groups of people, including adults and children, to work together harmoniously.**

You will find suggestions for *Look, listen and note*, *Effective practice* and *Planning and resourcing* in the EYFS Practice Guidance.

Personal, Social and Emotional Development

Personal, Social and Emotional Development
Making Relationships (30 – 50 months)

Development matters	Play and practical support
Form friendships with other children.	At this age and stage, children define 'friends' simply as 'children I have played with'. Therefore if you can encourage different combinations of children to play together, you will actually have encouraged them to see all these children as 'friends'.

Sample activity	Collecting Friends
What you need	A whiteboard or magnetic board. Two small snapshots of each child, sticky tac and dry-wipe pens.
How to prepare	Make a grid on your board with a line and a column for each child. Mount the photos of the children along the top and down the side.
What to do	Show the children your grid at group time. Explain that you are going to have a special day collecting friends! See how many friends you can play with today. Towards the end of the session, make sure you meet up with each child and go over to the grid together. Talk about who they have played with and what they did and enter a tick (if using a whiteboard) or a magnetic counter (if using a magnetic board).
	Over the course of a week, encourage each child to spend some time playing with every other so that they will have collected the full 'pack of friends'! Give special stickers whenever children collect the 'pack' – 'I've made lots of friends this week'.
	The grid, in fact, provides you with a simple sociometric record of who interacts with whom, day by day.
Note	Keep a record of who each child plays with and their choices of play activity. Look out for any children who might be feeling isolated and encourage closer friendships for them.
Things to say	• Who did you play with today? • What did you do together? • What did you like best? • How did . . . feel when that happened?
Comments	

Personal, Social and Emotional Development

Personal, Social and Emotional Development
Making Relationships (40 – 60+ months)

Code: PSED 3

Development matters	Play and practical support
Work as part of a group or class, taking turns and sharing fairly, understanding that there needs to be agreed values and codes of behaviour for groups of people, including adults and children, to work together harmoniously.	Look for playing opportunities which involve partners and turn-taking, such as balloon catch or blowing and popping bubbles. Pair new starters with children who are already settled at the group for their first few sessions.

Sample activity	**Partner Pickle**
What you need	Safe places to hide. If you are playing indoors, the usual barriers and screens of your play space will probably make spaces to hide behind. If you are outdoors, you may have to create spaces within your safety area; 'dens', tented climbing frames, a crawling tunnel, large cardboard boxes etc.
How to prepare	Set up some hiding places where a few children can fit in together. Arrange for an additional helper to provide general safety supervision.
What to do	This is a variation of the party game 'sardines'. Tell the children you are going to play a hiding game. Allow them to choose another friend to play it with, and help to ensure your quieter children play too. Challenge the 'partners' to see if they can stay holding hands the whole game. Take them on a tour around the play area, showing them the bounds and suggesting some good hiding places. Choose one pair to be the hiders. Count slowly and loudly to ten whilst the others turn their backs and hide their eyes. When a pair of seekers find the couple hiding, they hide there too, joining hands with the others. Once you have taught the game, stand back and allow the children to develop it in their own way. By making turn-taking part of a social game, you can teach social rules in a way that makes it fun and meaningful.
Note	Observe whether the children can grasp the concept of 'my turn, your turn' by taking it in turns to be hiders and seekers.
Things to say	• Where will you hide next? • How will you decide whose turn it is next?
Comments	

Personal, Social and Emotional Development

Personal, Social and Emotional Development

Behaviour and Self-control

Development Matters

30 – 50 months
- Begin to accept the needs of others, with support.
- Show care and concern for others, for living things and the environment.

40 – 60+ months
- Show confidence and the ability to stand up for own rights.
- Have an awareness of the boundaries set, and of behavioural expectations in the setting.
- **Understand what is right, what is wrong, and why.**
- **Consider the consequences of their words and actions for themselves and others.**

You will find suggestions for *Look, listen and note*, *Effective practice* and *Planning and resourcing* in the EYFS Practice Guidance.

Personal, Social and Emotional Development

Personal, Social and Emotional Development
Behaviour and Self-control (30 – 50 months)

Code: PSED 4

Development matters	Play and practical support
Show care and concern for others, for living things and the environment.	Look for natural opportunities throughout the session to talk about caring for each other and your resources.

Sample activity	At the Vets
What you need	Soft toy animals and resources to make a vet themed area in your play space – 'medical' equipment, blankets, dressings, pet carrying box, dishes, a low table, tissues, etc.
How to prepare	First of all, arrange a rota of visitors with their pets. Perhaps have one at the end of each session for a few days. Talk with the families first so that you are clear about any safety, allergy or hygiene considerations.
What to do	Introduce the visitors, and help the children to frame their questions so that they find out as much as possible about the pet and what is needed to look after it. Find out if the pet ever went to the Vet and why. Then set up the themed area with the children's help, asking them what they might need to play at being Vets. Having set this up, stand back and allow their play to develop. There is a helpful CD resource from Child's Eye Media on *People who help us* (www.childseyemedia.com) – see Number 2 for activities and resources connected with 'Vets'.
Note	Observe how the children respond to the pets when they visit and how they carry through their ideas about caring into their imaginative play.
Things to say	• Why did you choose a dog for a pet? How often does he need a walk? • What does your cat eat? Why doesn't she run away? • Where do chinchillas come from? • How did you train your guide dog?
Comments	

Personal, Social and Emotional Development

Personal, Social and Emotional Development
Behaviour and Self-control (40 – 60+ months)

Development matters	Play and practical support
Understand what is right, what is wrong, and why.	If children's behaviour is inappropriate, use stories and puppet play to illustrate the reasons why different behaviours might be right or wrong.

Sample activity	But it's Mine!
What you need	Three soft toys. A bag for one of the soft toys and a small sweet to go in it.
How to prepare	Ask a small group of children to help you get ready for a story. Can they help you choose three of the soft toys to take part? Which one shall your story be about? Which one should be the kind one? Which one shall be the naughty one? What shall we call them? Ask any child who you are particularly targeting to hold on to the kind one for the first part of the story.
What to do	Gather the children in a circle, sitting on the floor. Introduce the three soft toys and ask your young helper to tell the children their names. Place the little bag around the main character of your story, showing the children what is inside it. Tell a story of the toy walking to nursery one day, making it do the actions. Talk about what it sees on its way as it looks all around and stops to admire the birds flying overhead and the clear blue sky. But oh dear! The naughty toy is coming up and putting its paw into the bag. It's going to steal the sweet! It's running away! The first toy decides to stop to have a snack. But the sweet is gone? You might follow up with a discussion about what the children can take home (pictures, models, toys they have asked to borrow) and those they can't (other children's belongings, the Lego or cars, etc.).
Note	Collect samples of a child's questions or explanations which will help you interpret what they understand about right and wrong.
Things to say	• What will it feel like now? Look! It's crying. • Was it right to take the sweet? Why? • Encourage the child holding the 'kind' toy to make suggestions about how it will comfort and help the one that is crying. • Help the children make suggestions about what the 'naughty' toy can do to say 'sorry'.
Comments	

Personal, Social and Emotional Development

Code: PSED 5

Personal, Social and Emotional Development

Self-care

Development Matters

30 – 50 months
- Show willingness to tackle problems and enjoy self-chosen challenges.
- Demonstrate a sense of pride in own achievement.
- Take initiatives and manage developmentally appropriate tasks.

40 – 60+ months
- Operate independently within the environment and show confidence in linking up with others for support and guidance.
- Appreciate the need for hygiene.
- **Dress and undress independently and manage their own personal hygiene.**
- **Select and use activities and resources independently.**

You will find suggestions for *Look, listen and note*, *Effective practice* and *Planning and resourcing* in the EYFS Practice Guidance.

Personal, Social and Emotional Development

Personal, Social and Emotional Development
Self-care (30 – 50 months)

Development matters	Play and practical support
Demonstrate a sense of pride in own achievement.	Throughout the session give time and space to celebrate the children's interests, focusing on process rather than product.

Sample activity	I Belong
What you need	A large panel of paper, paints, glue, collage materials, photographs or self-portraits of the children, old toy catalogues and magazines, scissors.
How to prepare	Wait until your group has a special birthday or anniversary. Mount the panel of paper across one wall to form the basis of a huge celebration frieze. Have it low enough for the children to help mount or inspect their own contributions. Set up an art, collage and cutting table near to it.
What to do	Tell the children about the coming occasion, and explain that you are going to make a huge picture to celebrate. The picture is going to be all about themselves, the things they have learned to do and the activities they like doing in the group. Think of a unifying theme – perhaps each child could fill in one of a bunch of balloons, or one leaf of a branch, or one piece of a giant jig-saw. Each contribution could include a photograph or self-portrait of the child, cuttings-out of favourite toys and activities from the toy catalogue, or a collage of precious materials which the child has chosen to stick on. Encourage all your adults to do this too. Involve the children themselves in the idea of the theme for the frieze, and in helping to make the background of the frieze exciting too. Enjoy a birthday or anniversary celebration on the day, and declare your frieze officially open!
Note	Observe children's reactions to what they have achieved and how closely they identify with the group.
Things to say	• Take time to talk about the choices the children are making for their contributions, respecting and valuing their ideas. • Look for common themes with other children represented in the frieze and point these out.
Comments	

Personal, Social and Emotional Development

Personal, Social and Emotional Development
Self-care (40 – 60+ months)

Development matters	Play and practical support
Dress and undress independently and manage their own personal hygiene.	Arrival and departure times are an important part of your session and provide natural opportunities to support self-help skills.

Sample activity	Wrapping Up
What you need	All the children's outdoor clothing including coats and jackets, with fastenings undone. A CD player with lively music.
How to prepare	Before it is time to go outside on a cold day, collect the coats together in the centre of a large space.
What to do	Tell the children you are going to play a musical dressing game. When they hear the music, they can dance. When it stops, they can try to find their own outdoor clothes quickly and put them on. Tell them you will be there to help them. When the music starts again they must dance again! Continue until everyone is ready to go out. Give your constant praise and encouragement for their efforts, however much help they need. Encourage younger children to put arms into sleeves or pull up a zip, even if you are doing the rest. Make the game more difficult for older children by turning their jackets inside out!
Note	Note down how independent each child is in their dressing skills and what support they still need. This will help you to provide just the right amount of help and no more.
Things to say	• Who else has a coat this colour? • Introduce the words 'up', 'down', 'inside out'. • Can you turn it round/right side out (etc.)? • Talk about keeping warm. When do we put coats on?
Comments	

Personal, Social and Emotional Development

Code: PSED 6

Personal, Social and Emotional Development

Sense of Community

Development Matters

30 – 50 months
- Make connections between different parts of their life experience.

40 – 60+ months
- Have an awareness of, and an interest in, cultural and religious differences.
- Have a positive self-image, and show that they are comfortable with themselves.
- Enjoy joining in with family customs and routines.
- **Understand that people have different needs, views, cultures and beliefs, that need to be treated with respect.**
- **Understand that they can expect others to treat their needs, views, cultures and beliefs with respect.**

You will find suggestions for *Look, listen and note*, *Effective practice* and *Planning and resourcing* in the EYFS Practice Guidance.

Personal, Social and Emotional Development

Personal, Social and Emotional Development
Sense of Community (30 – 50 months)

Development matters	Play and practical support
Make connections between different parts of their life experience.	Making personalised picture books about the children helps them to make sense of their experiences and gives them value.

Sample activity	This is My Life
What you need	A2 sugar paper in a variety of colours. A mirror to look in. Paper to draw on and cut, a range of crayons or felt tips, and paste. A selection of printed photographs of the child – perhaps with some scanned in from home as well. You will need a black felt-tip to write down each child's story.
How to prepare	Make up a scrap book of different coloured sugar paper for each child; about eight pages of A4 (folded from 2 sheets of A2) would be fine. Set up an activity table in a quiet corner of the group.
What to do	Tell the children that you are going to help them write a book all about themselves. Start by talking about how each child looks just like themselves and nobody else. Look in the mirror and talk about this. Encourage each child to draw a picture of themselves to stick on the front cover of the scrapbook, and choose a title together. Help to keep all the comments positive and show that you value each child's thoughts. Return to this activity at later sessions in order to complete pages on *my family*, *where I live*, *my favourite toys*, *things I like to do*, *my friends* in the group. Gradually build up the pages by mounting their collages or drawings, or by writing down what they ask you to. Keep the personalised books in the book corner for any child to get out, share or talk about. This will help them develop an interest and understanding in each other. Read them to the whole group if the children agree beforehand.
Note	Note how well each child can make sense of their personal experiences and the words they select for their narratives.
Things to say	• What do you want me to write about you? • What shall we put first? • Prompt by questioning if you need to: Who else is in your family?' (etc.)
Comments	

Personal, Social and Emotional Development

Personal, Social and Emotional Development
Sense of Community (40 – 60+ months)

Development matters	Play and practical support
Enjoy joining in with family customs and routines.	Once again if you can personalise the learning you will find that it is far more accessible to the children. In this activity, you need the help of parents and carers.

Sample activity	It Happened to Me
What you need	A parent or carer willing to help you by photographing a special celebration, ritual or custom at home.
How to prepare	Ask the parents or carer to take a series of photographs of the special event for you, showing their child in each frame.
What to do	Take time downloading the photographs onto your computer and finding out from parents what was going on in the correct sequence. Add a sentence of text to each photograph. Then print off the photographs and stick each onto card or laminate it. Punch a hole in one corner and treasury tag them together in the correct order. Rehearse with the child concerned their 'story' and then use the picture cards as a focus during group time to share information about that child's particular celebration, ritual or custom. Support the children as they ask interested questions. With the child and parents' consent, your collection of stories could become a regular resource in your book corner.
Note	Observe the child's reactions as she or he shares their story with others.
Things to say	• What was happening here? • What happened next? • Did you enjoy doing this? • Who else celebrates Divali; goes to the mosque; went to a Christingle service (etc.)?
Comments	

Personal, Social and Emotional Development

Area of Learning: Personal, Social and Emotional Development		
Focus:	**Age Range:**	**Code: PSED** _____

Development matters	Play and practical support

Sample activity	
What you need	
How to prepare	
What to do	
Note	
Things to say	
Comments	

Ⓟ

Completed by: **Date:**

Personal, Social and Emotional Development
(30–60+ months)

Date of activity:	Supervised by:
Children involved:	
Comments	

Date of activity:	Supervised by:
Children involved:	
Comments	

Date of activity:	Supervised by:
Children involved:	
Comments	

(P)

Communication, Language and Literacy

(30–60+ months)

Communication, Language and Literacy
(30–60+ months)

Section index

Sample Activities

	30 – 50 months	40 – 60+ months
CLL 1 Language for Communication	Page 42	Page 43
CLL 2 Language for Thinking	Page 45	Page 46
CLL 3 Linking Sounds and Letters	Page 48	Page 49
CLL 4 Reading	Page 51	Page 52
CLL 5 Writing	Page 54	Page 55
CLL 6 Handwriting	Page 57	Page 58

A blank planner for you to copy and complete for the children is on page 59. There are also non-specific blank planners for you to copy and complete at the back of the book.
There is a monitoring sheet for you to use and adapt on page 60.

Communication, Language and Literacy

Language for Communication

Development Matters

30 – 50 months

- Use simple statements and questions often linked to gestures.
- Use intonation, rhythm and phrasing to make their meaning clear to others.
- Join in with repeated refrains and anticipate key events and phrases in rhymes and stories.
- Listen to stories with increasing attention and recall.
- Describe main story settings, events and principal characters.
- Listen to others in one-to-one or small groups when conversation interests them.
- Respond to simple instructions.
- Question why things happen and give explanations.
- Use vocabulary focused on objects and people that are of particular importance to them.
- Begin to experiment with language describing possession.
- Build up vocabulary that reflects the breadth of their experiences.
- Begin to use more complex sentences.
- Use a widening range of words to express or elaborate on ideas.

You will find suggestions for *Look, listen and note*, *Effective practice* and *Planning and resourcing* in the EYFS Practice Guidance.

Communication, Language and Literacy

Code: CLL 1

Communication, Language and Literacy

Language for Communication

Development Matters

40 – 60+ months

- Have confidence to speak to others about their own wants and interests.
- Use talk to gain attention and sometimes use action rather than talk to demonstrate or explain to others.
- Initiate conversation, attend to and take account of what others say.
- Extend vocabulary, especially by grouping and naming.
- Use vocabulary and forms of speech that are increasingly influenced by their experience of books.
- Link statements and stick to a main theme or intention.
- Consistently develop a simple story, explanation or line of questioning.
- Use language for an increasing range of purposes.
- Use simple grammatical structures.
- **Interact with others, negotiating plans and activities and taking turns in conversation.**
- **Enjoy listening to and using spoken and written language, and readily turn it to their play and learning.**
- **Sustain attentive listening, responding to what they have heard with relevant comments, questions or actions.**
- **Listen with enjoyment, and respond to stories, songs and other music, rhymes and poems.**
- **Extend their vocabulary, exploring the meanings and sounds of new words.**
- **Speak clearly and audibly with confidence and control and show awareness of the listener.**

You will find suggestions for *Look, listen and note*, *Effective practice* and *Planning and resourcing* in the EYFS Practice Guidance.

Communication, Language and Literacy

Communication, Language and Literacy
Language for Communication (30 – 50 months)

Development matters	Play and practical support
Begin to experiment with language describing possession.	Children's first use of possessives (such as 'mine') will come when they are playing naturally. However, you can also plan activities that are going to make their use more likely.

Sample activity	Feeling Good
What you need	A carpet to sit on. A teddy bear. Some of the activities need music. A 'magic wand'.
How to prepare	Plan your activities ahead (see below) so that you can present them smoothly.

What to do	Ask the children and all the adults to sit down in a circle and explain that it is 'circle time'. 'Warm up' by passing a teddy around, each one saying 'Hello' to it. Then choose some sentence completion activities from the list.
	  • **Favourite toys** – each child says what their favourite toy is, and why: '*My* best toy is . . . because . . .'
	  • **Animal friends** – each child thinks of an animal they would like to be, and chooses another child to be an animal friend. '*My* animal is . . ., *your* animal is . . . '. Then wave a wand, and both children 'become' the animal for a little while. Make sure everyone has a go. Join in with the less confident children.
	  • **Favourite foods** – each child is encouraged to think of something they really like to eat: '*My* favourite food is . . .'
	  • **Feeling faces** – each child takes it in turns to model an expression. '*My* face looks . . . (happy/sad/angry/etc.)' and encourage the rest to copy.
	  • **Introductions** – help each child to introduce their neighbour around the circle, and to say one thing about them that they like: 'This is Ahmed, and I like *his* smile'.
	You can use circle time to bring small 'family' groups together, to share ideas and plans, enjoy language and communication together and to round off the session.

Note	Keep a note of the possessive words that each child is beginning to use.
Things to say	• What does his/her/your/my face look like? • Is this *your* favourite too?
Comments	

Communication, Language and Literacy

Communication, Language and Literacy
Language for Communication (40 – 60+ months)   Code: CLL 1

Development matters	Play and practical support
Interact with others, negotiating plans and activities and taking turns in conversation.	Puppets are a wonderful resource for encouraging early conversations, especially with shy children or reluctant speakers.

Sample activity	Ring-a-ling
What you need	Two toy telephones and a large puppet.
How to prepare	No other preparation is needed.
What to do	Sit down with a small group of children and introduce your puppet. Explain that the puppet is very shy and she does not like to use the telephone. Encourage the children to tell him or her what to do. Make the puppet pretend to pick up the receiver and dial a number. Then tell one of the children 'It's for you!' Encourage the child to lift the receiver as the puppet says, rather tentatively, 'Hello? Who's there?' Encourage the child to say their name. The puppet then asks, 'Will you be my friend?' and, when the child replies, says goodbye. You can develop the conversations as the activity develops, making sure that each child is telephoned by the puppet. For example, in a second round of telephones, each child can telephone the puppet in turn and ask a question or hold a simple conversation. Praise the children for making the puppet feel so welcome. You can also use toy (or unused 'real') telephones in the role play area and encourage simple conversations as part of a game of 'offices' or 'doctor's surgery'.
Note	As you gradually make the activity more complex, note how well each child can respond to a simple conversation, maintain the conversation or even develop the conversation.
Things to say	• I think she's shy – try asking her her name. • Tell her what you're going to do next today. • Try asking her a question.
Comments	

Communication, Language and Literacy

Code: CLL 2

Communication, Language and Literacy

Language for Thinking

Development Matters

30 – 50 months
- Talk activities through, reflecting on and modifying what they are doing.
- Use talk to give new meanings to objects and actions, treating them as symbols for other things.
- Use talk to connect ideas, explain what is happening and anticipate what might happen next.
- Use talk, actions and objects to recall and relive past experiences.

40 – 60+ months
- Begin to use talk instead of action to rehearse, reorder and reflect on past experience, linking significant events from own experience and from stories, paying attention to how events lead into one another.
- Begin to make patterns in their experience through linking cause and effect, sequencing, ordering and grouping.
- Begin to use talk to pretend imaginary situations.
- **Use language to imagine and recreate roles and experiences.**
- **Use talk to organise, sequence and clarify thinking, ideas, feelings and events.**

You will find suggestions for *Look, listen and note*, *Effective practice* and *Planning and resourcing* in the EYFS Practice Guidance.

Communication, Language and Literacy

Communication, Language and Literacy
Language for Thinking (30 – 50 months)

Development matters	Play and practical support
Use talk to connect ideas, explain what is happening and anticipate what might happen next.	Help the children to use their developing language to anticipate by using natural opportunities throughout the session to ask 'what would happen if . . . ?' questions.

Sample activity	Story Chains
What you need	Cards, pens and scissors to make story sequences.
How to prepare	Make a sequence of three of four pictures which, in the correct order, would suggest an obvious story. For example, your four cards could have simple pictures of: 1. Child is fast asleep in bed. Curtains are drawn. 2. Child is in pyjamas washing face. 3. Child is dressed and having breakfast. 4. Child is wrapped up and walking out the door with Mum.
What to do	Sit on the floor or at a table with a small group of children and show them the cards. Present them one at a time, but not in their correct order. Once you have talked about a picture, place it on the table so that the children can still see it. Once you have all four laid out, invite the children to arrange the cards in the right order, with everyone helping. Encourage them to lay the cards from left to right across the table. Now invite the children to retell you the story as it happened, pointing to each picture in turn. Make more story chains yourselves and talk about them together as you arrange them. Sometimes children with language difficulties have difficulties in understanding sequences. If so, be ready to help them put their thoughts into words and to remember them long enough to sequence the pictures.
Note	This will give you plenty of opportunity for listening to the children's explanations and whether they are able to anticipate events.
Things to say	• What do you think is happening in this picture? • I wonder what happened before? • What is going to happen next?
Comments	

Communication, Language and Literacy

Communication, Language and Literacy
Language for Thinking (40 – 60+ months)

Development matters	Play and practical support
Use language to imagine and recreate roles and experiences.	Just provide exciting resources and opportunities – and the rest should follow!

Sample activity	Magic Carpet
What you need	A large mat which you can all sit on together: this could be a floor rug or a P.E. safety mat. Individual mats made of carpet squares or sheets of thick paper which the children have decorated themselves, one for each child. An open space.
How to prepare	Place your large mat in a suitable non-slip space.
What to do	Gather the children on the large mat for a game of pretend. Wouldn't it be wonderful if your carpet could fly! Shall we pretend? Sit tight as you invent some magic words to say. Chant them together and provide a running commentary as you all hang on tight. You are flying this way (all lean to the left) and that way (all lean to the right). Oh no! Now it's bumpy! What can the children see down below? Develop the game as the children come up with their own ideas and make sure you land safely. Suggest that the children have their own magic carpets, and encourage each child to place their small mat in a space and sit on it as your story continues. Finish with a final trip together on the big mat, repeating all your adventures in reverse as you fly all the way home. Encourage some of the children to retell their magic carpet story for you to write down with them and ask them to illustrate it.
Note	Keep an ear open for short samples of the children's language that let you know they are using it imaginatively, flexibly and creatively.
Things to say	• What can you see below you now? • Oh no – look what's coming! • Where shall we fly to next? • What do you think we'll find there?
Comments	

Communication, Language and Literacy

Code: CLL 3

Communication, Language and Literacy

Linking Sounds and Letters

Development Matters

30 – 50 months
- Enjoy rhyming and rhythmic activities.
- Show awareness of rhyme and alliteration.
- Recognise rhythm in spoken words.

40 – 60+ months
- Continue a rhyming string.
- Hear and say the initial sound in words and know which letters represent some of the sounds.
- **Hear and say sounds in words in the order in which they occur.**
- **Link sounds to letters, naming and sounding the letters of the alphabet.**
- **Use their phonic knowledge to write simple regular words and make phonetically plausible attempts at more complex words.**

You will find suggestions for *Look, listen and note*, *Effective practice* and *Planning and resourcing* in the EYFS Practice Guidance.

Communication, Language and Literacy

Communication, Language and Literacy
Linking Sounds and Letters (30 – 50 months)

Development matters	Play and practical support
Enjoy rhyming and rhythmic activities.	Singing and rhyming can make the learning of letter sounds intrinsically more motivating and enjoyable.

Sample activity	**The Buzzy Bee Game**
What you need	A series of cards and a felt-tip pen.
How to prepare	Write a single large letter on each card, selecting the letter sounds you are going to practise. To start with, you will need 'z', 'b', 'm', 'l', 's', 'o', 'f' and 'g'.
What to do	Gather a group of children together and teach them the Buzzy Bee song to the tune of 'Twinkle twinkle little star' *Listen to the buzzy bee! Make the sound and sing with me* *zz-zz-zz-zz-zz-zz-zz! zz-zz-zz-zz-zz-zz-zz!* *Listen to the buzzy bee! Make the sound and sing with me.* Sing the sounds slowly. The point about this song is that you can adapt it to suit most sounds that you wish to practise. Don't be afraid to use your imagination even if the song no longer scans! You might add: Listen to the woolly sheep! (b-b-b-b-b-b-baa), Listen to the farmer's cow! (m-m-m-m-m-m-moo), Listen to the singing birds! (la-la-la-la-la-la-la), Listen to the slithery snake! (ss-ss-ss-ss-ss-ss-ss), Grandad's gone and banged his toe (o-o-o-o-o-o-oh), Watch the engine puffing home (f-f-f-f-f-f-fuh) or even Mummy's trying to start her car (g-g-g-g-g-g-guh)! As you sing each verse, hold up the card showing the letter sound. Once they are familiar with the rhyme, you can place the letter cards on the floor and invite children to come out and select the correct letter as you sing. In time, you can hold up a letter card, ask the children what sound it makes and then sing the verse that goes with that sound.
Note	Observe whether the use of singing and rhyming helps to engage certain children better in playing with letter sounds. Which letters can they say/match/recognise/identify?
Things to say	• Can we think of a verse to go with 't'? • Is this card an 's'? Or this one? • Let's trace the shape and say the sound.
Comments	

Communication, Language and Literacy

Communication, Language and Literacy
Linking Sounds and Letters (40 – 60+ months)

Code: CLL 3

Development matters	Play and practical support
Link sounds to letters, naming and sounding the letters of the alphabet.	Picture alphabet friezes are so memorable and help children link sounds and images – mount one in your washing area or book corner so that it becomes really familiar.

Sample activity	I Spy, you Spy
What you need	Six familiar objects with clear consonant word beginnings, such as a cup, a brick, a train, a lollipop, a (toy) dog and a glove. Six cards (about A5 size) and pens.
How to prepare	Write the initial letter of each of the objects on one side of a card. In the example above, you will have six cards for 'c', 'b', 't', 'l', 'd' and 'g'. On the other side of each card, draw a picture of the object you have chosen.
What to do	Gather a small group of children in a circle, sitting on the floor. Place the six objects and the six cards, letter side up, on the floor in the centre. Invite one child to choose one of the objects and to whisper it to you. Talk quietly to the child and ask what sound that object begins with, prompting if you need to. Once you have decided together what the initial sound is, tell all the children that (child's name) has chosen something which begins with . . . , asking your young helper to tell all the other children the initial sound. Invite children to guess what the object is, and also to identify the written letter which makes that sound. Repeat for all the objects and sounds, with the same 'helper' or taking turns. Once the children have become used to the pictures, cards and sounds, you can dispense with the objects and use the cards to help the child remember their letter sounds. Show the card with the letter showing. If the child cannot remember what it says, they can turn the card over and remember the initial sound of the picture. You can link your pictures and sounds into any particular phonics scheme you are using.
Note	You should gradually be able to observe each child becoming familiar with a wider range of letter sounds and shapes.
Things to say	• Which thing/picture begins with a 'l' (etc)? – then emphasise each word for comparison. • Who has a 'j' in their name? (etc) • Look, we can make a word with these letters – you try too!
Comments	

Communication, Language and Literacy •

Code: CLL 4

Communication, Language and Literacy

Reading

Development Matters

30 – 50 months

- Listen and join in with stories and poems, one-to-one and also in small groups.
- Begin to be aware of the way stories are structured.
- Suggest how the story might end.
- Show interest in illustrations and print in books and print in the environment.
- Handle books carefully.
- Know information can be relayed in the form of print.
- Hold books the correct way up and turn pages.
- Understand the concept of a word.

40 – 60+ months

- Enjoy an increasing range of books.
- Know that information can be retrieved from books and computers.
- **Explore and experiment with sounds, words and texts.**
- **Retell narratives in the correct sequence, drawing on language patterns of stories.**
- **Read a range of familiar and common words and simple sentences independently.**
- **Know that print carries meaning and, in English, is read from left to right and top to bottom.**
- **Show an understanding of the elements of stories, such as main character, sequence of events and openings, and how information can be found in non-fiction texts to answer questions about where, who, why and how.**

You will find suggestions for *Look, listen and note*, *Effective practice* and *Planning and resourcing* in the EYFS Practice Guidance.

Communication, Language and Literacy

Communication, Language and Literacy
Reading (30 – 50 months)

Development matters	Play and practical support
Know information can be relayed in the form of print.	Copy a range of familiar signs and notices around the room so the children can talk about where they usually appear and what they mean.

Sample activity	Good Report
What you need	A CD recorder/dictaphone or cassette tape recorder. Paper, pens and pencils. A3 sheets and glue. A selection of newspapers (carefully filleted!).
How to prepare	Arrange everything in a corner of your space – this is your 'news desk'.
What to do	Gather some of the children together and show them your newspaper. Talk about what they are for and what they tell you. Share an idea of putting together a newspaper for the parents and carers and collect ideas from all the children. Think of a suitable title for it together. Show them how to use the recorders. Suggest that each child takes it in turns to put something on the tape for you to write into the newspaper, and draws a picture to go with it. Support them as they put their thoughts into practice. As the session progresses, encourage each child to stay beside you as you listen to their words on the tape and you write them onto a large A3 sheet of 'newspaper'. Glue in their picture beneath their words. Later you can take A3 photocopies of your newspaper for each child to take home. Older children can attempt their own simple report writing or copying.
Note	Use your initial discussion to observe what the children already understand about printed material such as newspapers.
Things to say	• What is a newspaper for? • What does it tell you? • If we wanted to tell people all about our group, what things could we put in our own newspaper?
Comments	

Communication, Language and Literacy
Reading (40 – 60+ months)   Code: CLL 4

Development matters	Play and practical support
Read a range of familiar and common words and simple sentences independently.	Much of children's early word recognition comes from seeing familiar words and patterns of words around them. Label everything simply and clearly – especially real photographs of the children at play.

Sample activity	Gone Fishing
What you need	A4 coloured and white card, scissors, felt-tip pens, glue, metallic paper clips, a length of thin dowel about 30 cm long, string and a small magnet. A blue mat or similar.
How to prepare	Outline in thick pen and cut out a familiar shape from each coloured card – a fish, a boot, a car, a teapot, a hat perhaps. Then make two sets of identical labels for your items in white card, so that they fit within the outline – write on 'fish', 'boot, 'car', 'teapot', 'hat' (etc.). Stick one set to the corresponding shape. You now have one set of labelled shapes and one identical set of separate labels. Attach paper clips to all of these. Make simple 'fishing lines' out of your doweling and string, each with a small magnet in place of a hook.
What to do	Sit down with some of the children and arrange all the labelled shapes onto your blue mat or sheet to represent 'the sea'. Arrange the word cards on the 'land' nearby. Show them how they can use the rod to 'catch' things in the sea. As each child catches something, encourage them to tell you what it is and then to 'catch' the corresponding label. Encourage the children to take turns until all the fish are caught. As a next stage, arrange the label cards in the sea and encourage the children to catch something you have named for them. Finally, encourage them to fish for words and then tell you what that word says. You can play a similar game with simple sentences – simply draw a simple illustration/use a photograph with a simple sentence beneath such as 'Tammy is running'. As before, at first fish for the picture and later the sentence on its own.
Note	This activity allows you to differentiate between children associating the written word with the shape, identifying the word when you name it and finally reading it on their own.
Things to say	• Catch me a boot if you can! • What sound does it begin with? • Let's trace that letter in the sea . . .
Comments	

Communication, Language and Literacy

Code: CLL 5

Communication, Language and Literacy

Writing

Development Matters

30 – 50 months
- Sometimes give meaning to marks as they draw and paint.
- Ascribe meanings to marks that they see in different places.

40 – 60+ months
- Begin to break the flow of speech into words.
- Use writing as a means of recording and communicating.
- **Use their phonic knowledge to write simple regular words and make phonetically plausible attempts at more complex words.**
- **Attempt writing for different purposes, using features of different forms such as lists, stories and instructions.**
- **Write their own names and other things such as labels and captions, and begin to form simple sentences, sometimes using punctuation.**

You will find suggestions for *Look, listen and note*, *Effective practice* and *Planning and resourcing* in the EYFS Practice Guidance.

Communication, Language and Literacy

Communication, Language and Literacy
Writing (30 – 50 months)

Development matters	Play and practical support
Ascribe meanings to marks that they see in different places.	Introduce simple signs and marks to act as indications in your play space – arrows for tracks, lines for trails, 'no entry' for your bike area, simple tally counts for how many children can climb on the frame, etc.

Sample activity	Trail Trackers
What you need	A hard outdoor play surface, plenty of obstacles to hide behind and a selection of coloured chalks, short sticks (or pipe cleaners or coloured spills) and pebbles.
How to prepare	Before the children arrive, set up a trail. Use one colour of chalk and also your sticks and arrangements of pebbles to make arrows. Spread them out a bit to make it challenging. Arrange for one of the helpers to be hiding at the end of the trail.
What to do	Start off with a small group of children outside. Show them the first arrow and ask them to work out with you what is happening. As the children discover more signs and marks, encourage them to follow and to search for more. Eventually they should discover your colleague! Now show the children how they can use the chalks to leave their own tracks and marks. Help them take it in turns to follow the tracks – each child using a differently coloured chalk to keep them distinct. Now stand back and let the game develop. If you ever have the chance of group trip to the beach, this makes a wonderful game to play in the sand – bury a fancy shell at the end of the trail.
Note	Observe the marks and signs that the children develop for themselves and the meanings they ascribe to them.
Things to say	• Which way is it pointing? • Where next? • Will you make a track for me to follow?
Comments	

Communication, Language and Literacy

Communication, Language and Literacy
Writing (40 – 60+ months)

Development matters	Play and practical support
Attempt writing for different purposes, using different forms such as lists, stories and instructions.	Themed areas give children real reasons for wanting to use their early mark-making and writing skills for a variety of purposes which are fun and engaging.

Sample activity	At the Post Office
What you need	Everything you can think up to set up a post office counter – letters, envelopes, stickers (for stamps), rubber stamps and ink pads, parcels to wrap, posting box, pretend money, forms to fill in etc.
How to prepare	Set up a 'post office' area complete with counter and writing table for writing letters and wrapping parcels.
What to do	Spend some time talking about post offices or even visiting one and gathering photographs of your experience there. Discuss all the things that happen at post offices and how people there can help. Start by playing alongside some of the children as you pretend to write letters, address the envelopes, wrap parcels and decide who to 'send' them to. You might decide to 'send' your nursery Bear on its holidays and set up a regular correspondence between Bear and the children. In this way, you might find yourselves writing letters, lists of things for Bear to do and many different kinds of written communication, either via mark-making or with the children's early efforts at independent copying or writing. You can also encourage children to borrow Bear if they are spending a time in hospital or on holiday so that the children can write to Bear and she or he can reply.
Note	Observe the different forms of writing that each child engages in and the meanings ascribed to them.
Things to say	• Here's a postcard from Bear – this time we've got to reply to Brazil! • Bear needs us to send a book . . . • Tell me about your letter . . . what does it say?
Comments	

Communication, Language and Literacy

Code: CLL 6

Communication, Language and Literacy

Handwriting

Development Matters

30 – 50 months
- Use one-handed tools and equipment.
- Draw lines and circles using gross motor movements.
- Manipulate objects with increasing control.

40 – 60+ months
- Begin to use anticlockwise movement and retrace vertical lines.
- Begin to form recognisable letters.
- **Use a pencil and hold it effectively to form recognisable letters, most of which are correctly formed.**

You will find suggestions for *Look, listen and note*, *Effective practice* and *Planning and resourcing* in the EYFS Practice Guidance.

Communication, Language and Literacy

Communication, Language and Literacy
Handwriting (30 – 50 months)

Code: CLL 6

Development matters	Play and practical support
Draw lines and circles using gross motor movements.	Children start to master mark-making (and early letter formation) using their whole bodies and then refine the movements down later. You can make this fun by using slightly unusual media and materials.

Sample activity	Water Marks
What you need	Buckets of water, colouring (such as water-based paints), a selection of large brushes, paint brushes and rollers. You also need a hard (such as paved) area out of doors.
How to prepare	Involve the children in making up buckets of coloured water.
What to do	Move outdoors and show them how to 'paint' the ground with water. Encourage them to enjoy mark-making out of doors, experimenting with circular stepping stones and tracks between them using circular and straight brush strokes. However, they'll have to be quick – the water keeps disappearing! Paint rollers encourage beautifully straight lines and rows. Smaller brushes can be used for circular shapes. Stand back as their mark-making develops and have a mop ready for when the bucket inevitably gets spilt, watching out for slips. Follow up with large brush movements (this time using paints) on a vertical surface by creating a huge frieze together. You can also adapt this activity using real paints on a large sheet of paper or plastic sheet on the floor. In this way, children will enjoy the process of mark-making even more than the product.
Note	Note down examples of the children using their whole bodies to make circular and straight lines on the ground.
Things to say	• Quick – follow the track before it disappears! • Can you paint us some more stepping stones please? • Do we need a straight track to the door?
Comments	

Communication, Language and Literacy

Communication, Language and Literacy
Handwriting (40 – 60+ months)

Development matters	Play and practical support
Begin to form recognisable letters.	Keep your activities informal and playful so that the children enjoy the natural progression from early mark-making to correct letter formation.

Sample activity	Give Me a 'b'!
What you need	A shallow tray with a thin layer of dry sand. Sheets of paper and washable felt-tips. The Buzzy Bee rhyme on page 48.
How to prepare	No other preparation is needed.
What to do	Introduce this activity once you have become familiar with the Buzzy Bee rhyme. Sit down at a table with a small group of children and sing the song together as you work. Show the children how to write the letter for each verse, modelling the straight or circular movements in the air and then in the shallow sand tray, tracing them with your fingers. Once they are beginning to make the movements independently, encourage them to help you make cards for the verses of the song. Encourage the children to sound the letters or sing the verse with you as you form each letter. Finally, challenge the children to practise identifying the letters they have just written by chanting 'Give me an 'L'!' (saying the letter sound, not its name); 'give me a 'S'!' (etc.) and asking the children to hold up their cards. Keep it fun and motivating. If a child has difficulties in holding a pen or pencil correctly, use a triangular pen or grip to encourage the correct 'tripod' hold naturally.
Note	Use this as a natural opportunity to gradually build up each child's record of the letter sounds they can identify, name and form.
Things to say	• That 'b' looks like a bat and then a ball . . . • What does your name begin with? • Find me something else that begins with 't'.
Comments	

Communication, Language and Literacy

Area of Learning: Communication, Language and Literacy		
Focus:	Age Range:	Code: CLL _____
Development matters		**Play and practical support**

Sample activity	
What you need	
How to prepare	
What to do	
Note	
Things to say	
Comments	

Ⓟ

Completed by: **Date:**

Communication, Language and Literacy
(30–60+ months)

Date of activity:	Supervised by:
Children involved:	
Comments	

Date of activity:	Supervised by:
Children involved:	
Comments	

Date of activity:	Supervised by:
Children involved:	
Comments	

(P)

Problem Solving, Reasoning and Numeracy

(30–60+ months)

Problem Solving, Reasoning and Numeracy
(30–60+ months)

Section index

Sample Activities

		30 – 50 months	40 – 60+ months
PSRN 1	Numbers as labels and for counting	Page 66	Page 67
PSRN 2	Calculating	Page 69	Page 70
PSRN 3	Shape, Space and Measures	Page 73	Page 74

A blank planner for you to copy and complete for the children is on page 75. There are also non-specific blank planners for you to copy and complete at the back of the book.
There is a monitoring sheet for you to use and adapt on page 76.

Problem Solving, Reasoning and Numeracy

Numbers as Labels and for Counting

Development Matters

30 – 50 months

- Use some number names and number language spontaneously.
- Show curiosity about numbers by offering comments or asking questions.
- Use some number names accurately in play.
- Sometimes match number and quantity correctly.
- Recognise groups with one, two or three objects.

You will find suggestions for *Look, listen and note*, *Effective practice* and *Planning and resourcing* in the EYFS Practice Guidance.

Problem Solving, Reasoning and Numeracy

Code: PSRN 1

Problem Solving, Reasoning and Numeracy

Numbers as Labels and for Counting

Development Matters

40 – 60+ months

- Recognise some numerals of personal significance.
- Count up to three or four objects by saying one number name for each item.
- Count out up to six objects from a larger group.
- Count actions or objects that cannot be moved.
- Begin to count beyond 10.
- Begin to represent numbers using fingers, marks on paper or pictures.
- Select the correct numeral to represent 1 to 5.
- Count an irregular arrangement of up to ten objects.
- Estimate how many objects are in a set.
- Use ordinal numbers in different contexts.
- Match then compare the number of objects in two sets.
- **Say and use number names in order in familiar contexts.**
- **Count reliably up to ten everyday objects.**
- **Recognise numerals 1 to 9.**
- **Use developing mathematical ideas and methods to solve practical problems.**

You will find suggestions for *Look, listen and note*, *Effective practice* and *Planning and resourcing* in the EYFS Practice Guidance.

Problem Solving, Reasoning and Numeracy

Problem Solving, Reasoning and Numeracy
Numbers as Labels and for Counting (30 – 50 months)

Development matters	Play and practical support
Sometimes match number and quantity correctly.	Provide opportunities for the children to do this naturally and in playful situations so that they do not come to see early Number as something they can get 'right' or 'wrong'.

Sample activity	Countdown Challenge!
What you need	A hoop and ten coloured beanbags (or other objects which are easy to count). A set of four cards, each with the numeral '1' to '4' written on them. A football rattle or party whistle.
How to prepare	Gather a small group of children together – this activity works well out of doors. Suggest that you play a counting game. Place the hoop on the ground and arrange four number cards for '1', '2', '3' and '4' on the ground as well, numeral side up. Older children will be able to help you make the number cards.
What to do	Start with one of the older children. Place two beanbags in the circle and invite them to find the correct number card and place it in the circle with the beanbags. Cheer their success and wave your rattle. Let each child have a turn until all the beanbags end up in the hoops with the matching numeral card. Let the younger children go last so that there is less choice for them – this way they are bound to experience success! Next time around, give each child a number card and invite them to place the correct number of beanbags into the hoop. Again, cheer their success. You can gradually increase the numbers in the sets and the range of number cards you are matching. You will be able to choose a task at the right level of ability for each child, extending the set to twenty for the older children if you need to!
Note	As you gradually challenge each child more, observe whether they can count spontaneously and whether they have begun to match quantity to numeral.
Things to say	• How many now? • How many if I take one away from the hoop? • And if I add one more again? See if you can match the number now.
Comments	

Problem Solving, Reasoning and Numeracy

Problem Solving, Reasoning and Numeracy
Numbers as Labels and for Counting (40 – 60+ months)

Development matters	Play and practical support
Estimate how many objects they can see and check by counting them.	Encouraging children to help with the laying out and the putting away provides plenty of natural opportunities for counting and checking.

Sample activity	Tally Counts
What you need	Pieces of card (about 10 cm square), a felt-tip pen, a clip board and pencil for each child, sheets of A4 paper.
How to prepare	Make up about 10 cards in advance. On each one, decide on a familiar item in your nursery which could be easily counted. There should be no more then five of it at first, and ideally one of one thing, two of another (etc.). You might have one slide, two doors, three windows, four painting easels and five trucks. Draw a little picture of the items on each card and write on 'How many (name of item) can you count?' Clip a sheet of A4 paper onto each clip board and clip the card at the top.
What to do	Encourage each child to take a clip board and show them how they can count the items, making one stroke of their pencil to cancel out one of the pictures for each one they see. Choose cards which are going to be within each child's ability. Give each child several turns with different cards. When everyone has finished counting and marking, compare and check your results together, writing in the totals with your support. You can then provide older children with a card with just one picture at the top, for example a bike, and show them how to make a tally count to see how many bikes there are in the yard.
Note	This activity can be observed at several levels: – how well can each child count a group of objects? (counting sets) – can they still do this if those objects are spread out in different parts of the nursery? (counting plus memory) – can they record their findings?
Things to say	• How many bikes can you see? • Can you find the three light switches?
Comments	

Problem Solving, Reasoning and Numeracy

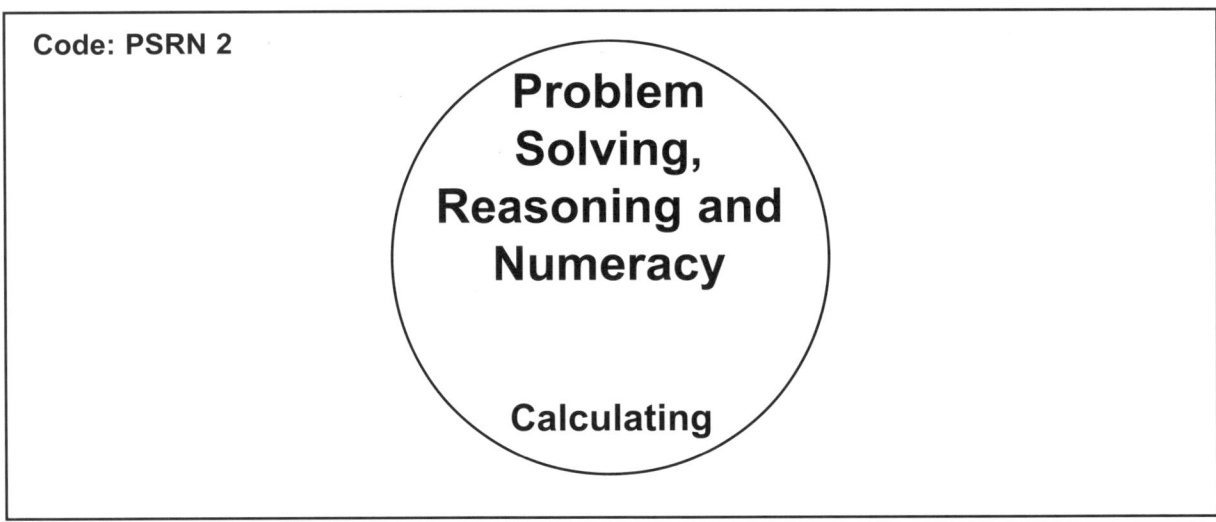

Code: PSRN 2

Problem Solving, Reasoning and Numeracy

Calculating

Development Matters

30 – 50 months

- Compare two groups of objects, saying when they have the same number.
- Show an interest in number problems.
- Separate a group of three or four objects in different ways, beginning to recognise that the total is still the same.

40 – 60+ months

- Find the total number of items in two groups by counting all of them.
- Use own methods to work through a problem.
- Say the number that is one more than a given number.
- Select two groups of objects to make a given total of objects.
- Count repeated groups of the same size.
- Share objects into equal groups and count how many in each group.
- **In practical activities and discussion, begin to use the vocabulary involved in adding and subtracting.**
- **Use language such as 'more' or 'less' to compare two numbers.**
- **Find one more or one less than a number from one to ten.**
- **Begin to relate addition to combining two groups of objects and subtraction to 'taking away'.**

You will find suggestions for *Look, listen and note*, *Effective practice* and *Planning and resourcing* in the EYFS Practice Guidance.

Problem Solving, Reasoning and Numeracy

Problem Solving, Reasoning and Numeracy
Calculating (30 – 50 months)

Code: PSRN 2

Development matters	Play and practical support
Compare two groups of objects, saying when they have the same number.	Sets of *children* are fun and meaningful to count when you are first learning about 'more' and 'less'.

Sample activity	**Nuts in May**
What you need	A large space.
How to prepare	No other preparation is needed.
What to do	Divide the children into two lines, with at least one adult in each line. Arrange for the two lines to face each other, about 10 metres apart. Encourage the children to take a part in sorting themselves out – this in itself provides a great learning opportunity! Hold hands in your rows. One line starts by singing the first verse of the traditional song which goes to the tune of 'Here we go round the mulberry bush'. *Here we come gathering nuts in May, nuts in May, nuts in May.* *Here we come gathering nuts in May, on a cold and frosty morning.* The other line then replies: *Who will you have for your nuts in May, nuts in May, nuts in May?* *Who will you have for your nuts in May on a cold and frosty morning?* The first line then gathers together in a huddle and chooses a child's name from the other group. *We will have (child's name) for our nuts in May, nuts in May, nuts in May.* *We will have (child's name) for our nuts in May on a cold and frosty morning.* Encourage the named child to join the first side. Now the second line starts the song. They could ask for two children if they like. Again, you can stop, ask the children to estimate and count the heads together. This traditional dance used to be sung with movement as well. Each side moves forwards and back as they sing their verse.
Note	How does each child recognise the concept of 'same number'? Does their judgement change when the rows are more spread out?
Things to say	• Which line has the *most* people now? • Do they have the *same* number now? • Which row has *less* people?
Comments	

Problem Solving, Reasoning and Numeracy

Problem Solving, Reasoning and Numeracy
Calculating (40 – 60+ months)

Development matters	Play and practical support
Share objects into equal groups and count how many in each group.	Certain play areas, such as a home corner or other themed area, lend themselves beautifully to sharing out and matching quantities. Use snack time as a natural opportunity for sharing out as well.

Sample activity	Tea for Two
What you need	Your usual home corner with kitchen equipment, cups, saucers, play food, dolls, beds, table, chairs, etc.
How to prepare	No other preparation is required.
What to do	Start by playing with one or two children (so long as you are invited!) in the home corner. Explain that you are feeling peckish and suggest that it would be wonderful if one of them could make tea for you all. Help them to put out plates, one for each person in the house. Use pointing to show the child who will have each plate so that you can help them work out how many are needed.
Do the same thing with the chairs round the table and with the saucers. Then help them to work out how many cups are needed for the saucers.
Share the food onto the plates, keeping the flow of the game as informal as possible. Look for natural opportunities to encourage the children to share out and to count.
As more children join the game, look for more chairs, plates, cups, etc. and count them out to check.
You might also involve the soft toys dolls and Bears.
Note	Keep it simple at first and observe whether a child can share out between, say, two children. Then observe how they can extend this further.
Things to say	• Do we need more or less plates and cups for everyone?
• Oh no – more teddies. How many more cups do we need?
• Look – Bear hasn't got as many as Panda . . .
Comments	

Problem Solving, Reasoning and Numeracy

Problem Solving, Reasoning and Numeracy

Space, Shape and Measures

Development Matters

30 – 50 months

- Show an interest in shape and space by playing with shapes or making arrangements with objects.
- Show awareness of similarities in shapes in the environment.
- Observe and use positional language.
- Are beginning to understand 'bigger than' and 'enough'.
- Show an interest in shape by sustained construction activity or by talking about shapes or arrangements.
- Use shapes appropriately for tasks.
- Begin to talk about the shapes of everyday objects.

You will find suggestions for *Look, listen and note*, *Effective practice* and *Planning and resourcing* in the EYFS Practice Guidance.

Problem Solving, Reasoning and Numeracy

Code: PSRN 3

Problem Solving, Reasoning and Numeracy

Space, Shape and Measures

40 – 60+ months

- Show curiosity about and observation of shapes by talking about how they are the same or different.
- Match some shapes by recognising similarities and orientation.
- Begin to use mathematical names for 'solid' 3D shapes and 'flat' 2D shapes, and mathematical terms to describe shapes.
- Select a particular named shape.
- Show awareness of symmetry.
- Find items from positional or directional clues.
- Order two or three items by length or height.
- Order two items by weight or capacity.
- Match sets of objects to numerals that represent the number of objects.
- Sort familiar objects to identify their similarities and differences, making choices and justifying decisions.
- Describe solutions to practical problems, drawing on experience, talking about own ideas, methods and choices.
- Use familiar objects and common shapes to create and recreate patterns and build models.
- Use everyday language related to time; order and sequence familiar events, and measure short periods of time with a non-standard unit, for example, with a sand timer.
- Count how many objects share a particular property, presenting results using pictures, drawings or numerals.
- **Use language such as 'greater', 'smaller', 'heavier' or 'lighter' to compare quantities.**
- **Talk about, recognise and recreate simple patterns.**
- **Use language such as 'circle' or 'bigger' to describe the shape and size of solids and flat shapes.**
- **Use everyday words to describe position.**
- **Use developing mathematical ideas and methods to solve practical problems.**

Problem Solving, Reasoning and Numeracy

Problem Solving, Reasoning and Numeracy
Shape, Space and Measures (30 – 50 months)

Development matters	Play and practical support
Show awareness of similarities in shapes in the environment.	You can encourage this by taking photographs of familiar surroundings and then emphasising familiar shapes by drawing over their outlines with a thick felt-tip pen.

Sample activity	All A-round
What you need	Large paper plates, sticky paper, paints and pens, cotton and sticky tape. A digital camera.
How to prepare	No other preparation is needed.
What to do	Gather some of the children together and show them one of the paper plates. Talk together about what shape it is. Use the words 'round' and 'circle'. Now invite the children to look around the room from where they are sitting and see if they can see anything else that is *round*. They might see a clock face, a plate of biscuits, a ball or hoop, the end of a paper roll, a door knob or a wheel. Now send them out around the room, inviting each child to come back and tell you about something *round* that they can see. Gather a few round objects together so that you can talk about them and photograph them. Finish by moving to a table and making round pictures onto the paper plates to represent what the children have seen. They might ask for help to draw a clock face, or they might stick paper shapes on to represent the plate of biscuits. Attach cotton to each round picture and suspend them from the ceiling to make a round mobile which twists and turns. Plan together how to make your photographs into a 'Round display'. You can also introduce solid three-dimensional shapes such as cylinders, cones, pyramids and cuboids. Encourage the children to manipulate them and count any *round* sides.
Note	Observe whether a child can generalise the 'roundness' that they see and handle in their plate with the roundness of objects around them.
Things to say	• Find me something else that is *round*. • Has it got a *round* edge? • That balloon picture looks like *circles*!
Comments	

Problem Solving, Reasoning and Numeracy

Problem Solving, Reasoning and Numeracy
Shape, Space and Measures (40 – 60+ months)

Development matters	Play and practical support
Find items from positional or directional clues.	Use your running commentary about what the children are doing to help them link positional and directional words with their actions at the time.

Sample activity	Over our Heads
What you need	A parachute (or cut an old double sheet into a circle), a large indoor or outdoor space and plenty of helpers.
How to prepare	Take off your shoes so that you are in your socks, slippers or plimsoles.
What to do	Show the children the parachute and encourage them to work out together how to hold onto an edge and make a big circle. When you have spaced yourself out around the parachute, sit down in a circle. Show the children how you can gently raise the parachute *high* and bring it down *low*. 'Sing' this chant with a rising and a falling voice. *We can go HIGH (pause for effect)* *We can go LOW (pause and repeat)* Now invite individual children to do different things. Ask the first child to crawl *over* the parachute until they join the circle at the other side. Ask the next to crawl *under*. You can also ask groups of named children to stay *under* or *on top* of the parachute as the rest of you make gentle waves for them. Then invite different children to choose the next child and say what they should do for their task. Invite others to identify children from the positions you give them. Finish by raising the parachute high and then all of you slipping underneath it as it falls gently onto you.
Note	Observe whether a child can follow the direction from the words you use alone or whether they need to copy someone else first.
Things to say	• *Where* do you want (child's name) to move to? • Who is *under* the parachute now? • Look who's *on top* of it now!
Comments	

Problem Solving, Reasoning and Numeracy

Area of Learning: Problem Solving, Reasoning and Numeracy		
Focus:	**Age Range:**	**Code: PSRN** _____
Development matters	**Play and practical support**	

Sample activity	
What you need	
How to prepare	
What to do	
Note	
Things to say	
Comments	

Ⓟ

Completed by: **Date:**

Problem Solving, Reasoning and Numeracy
(30–60+ months)

Date of activity:	Supervised by:
Children involved:	
Comments	

Date of activity:	Supervised by:
Children involved:	
Comments	

Date of activity:	Supervised by:
Children involved:	
Comments	

Ⓟ

Knowledge and Understanding of the World

(30–60+ months)

Knowledge and Understanding of the World
(30–60+ months)

Section index

Sample Activities

	30 – 50 months	40 – 60+ months
KUW 1 Exploration and Investigation	Page 81	Page 82
KUW 2 Designing and Making	Page 84	Page 85
KUW 3 ICT	Page 87	Page 88
KUW 4 Time	Page 90	Page 91
KUW 5 Place	Page 93	Page 94
KUW 6 Communities	Page 96	Page 97

A blank planner for you to copy and complete for the children is on page 98. There are also non-specific blank planners for you to copy and complete at the back of the book.
There is a monitoring sheet for you to use and adapt on page 99.

Code: KUW 1

Knowledge and Understanding of the World

Exploration and Investigation

Development Matters

30 – 50 months
- Show curiosity and interest in the features of objects and living things.
- Describe and talk about what they see.
- Show curiosity about why things happen and how things work.
- Show understanding of cause/effect relations.

40 – 60+ months
- Notice and comment on patterns.
- Show an awareness of change.
- Explain own knowledge and understanding, and ask appropriate questions of others.
- **Investigate objects and materials by using all of their senses as appropriate.**
- **Find out about, and identify, some features of living things, objects and events they observe.**
- **Look closely at similarities, differences, patterns and change.**
- **Ask questions about why things happen and how things work.**

You will find suggestions for *Look, listen and note*, *Effective practice* and *Planning and resourcing* in the EYFS Practice Guidance.

Knowledge and Understanding of the World

Knowledge and Understanding of the World
Exploration and Investigation (30 – 50 months)

Development matters	Play and practical support
Show understanding of cause/effect relations.	Look for natural opportunities to talk with the children about cause and effect – whether it is to do with objects and physical processes or with children and the effect they have on each other.

Sample activity	Domino Rally
What you need	Collect old video cases (or any like-sized items of a similar shape and weight). Chalk.
How to prepare	Try this activity out of doors on a level surface. You will be familiar with a 'domino rally' – where dominoes are stood vertically at exactly the right distance from each other so that when the first is pushed over it sets up a chain reaction and the rest gradually fall. The idea here is to try a similar experiment using larger objects which are easier to balance. Play around yourself until you have something that has an impressive effect. Mark where you have positioned the boxes with chalk and set it up ready for your display.
What to do	Gather some of the children to watch. See if they can predict what would happen if the first box fell over. Push it the wrong way . . . nothing much! Now set off your chain reaction by pushing it towards its neighbour. Talk about cause and effect and support the children as they recreate the experiment, eventually working out about the distances and using the chalk marks to help. Try it on different surfaces – does it make a difference? Try it with different shapes and sizes of objects – does that make a difference?
Note	Record general examples from the whole session of children being able to link causes and effects.
Things to say	• What will happen if . . . ? • Did this happen *because* of that? • I wonder why Jamie is crying? Can you help me work it out? • Oh look! Because (this has happened) (that has happened)!
Comments	

Knowledge and Understanding of the World

Knowledge and Understanding of the World
Exploration and Investigation (40 – 60+ months)

Development matters	Play and practical support
Find out about, and identify, some features of living things, objects and events they observe.	Always create opportunities for the children to ask questions and invest your personal time in answering them!

Sample activity	**Ice Cubes**
What you need	Food colouring, ice cube trays, novelty ice cube maker (if available, not essential), drinking water, plastic see-through tumblers and bowls, natural fruit juices, pieces of fruit. A tray for each child.
How to prepare	Make up some trays of ice cubes in advance. One tray should be colourless drinking water. Others can be drinking water coloured with different food dyes. Arrange the tumblers and bowls on the trays on top of a low table.
What to do	Invite some of the children to join you and help them wash and dry hands. Bring in a tray of colourless ice. Loosen the ice under a tap and empty the cubes onto the trays. Ask the children how they feel to touch as they slither and slide over the surface of the tray. Try to predict what will happen to the ice in the warm room. Encourage the children to place the ice in the glasses or bowls and place them in the sunshine or the shade, in a cool place or near the radiator. See whose ice melts first. Try adding ice cubes to a glass of warm water. Now bring in the coloured ice cubes and encourage the children to add them to glasses of clear water and watch the water change colour as the ice cubes melt. Finally, enjoy making fruity ice cubes together by placing small pieces of fruit in the ice tray, filling up with fruit juice and then freezing. Enjoy sucking these on a hot day.
Note	Ask individual children what they have found out from the activity.
Things to say	• What is ice made of? • What will happen to the ice in the warm room? • Whose ice is melting first? • What foods need to be kept in a fridge? Why does the door need to stay shut?
Comments	

Knowledge and Understanding of the World

Code: KUW 2

Knowledge and Understanding of the World

Designing and Making

Development Matters

30 – 50 months

- Investigate various construction materials.
- Realise tools can be used for a purpose.
- Join construction pieces together to build and balance.
- Begin to try out a range of tools and techniques safely.

40 – 60+ months

- Construct with a purpose in mind, using a variety resources.
- Use simple tools and techniques competently and appropriately.
- **Build and construct with a wide range of objects, selecting appropriate resources and adapting their work where necessary.**
- **Select the tools and techniques they need to shape, assemble and join materials they are using.**

You will find suggestions for *Look, listen and note*, *Effective practice* and *Planning and resourcing* in the EYFS Practice Guidance.

Knowledge and Understanding of the World

Knowledge and Understanding of the World
Designing and Making (30 – 50 months)

Code: KUW 2

Development matters	Play and practical support
Investigate various construction materials.	Outdoor spaces make excellent areas for large-scale construction and building activity. Make sure that there are always some resources on hand for building and den-making.

Sample activity	Building Bridges
What you need	A selection of building bricks and other solid shapes and resources in various shapes and sizes. A selection of small cars and trains.
How to prepare	Spread the resources on the floor in a clear space.
What to do	Invite some of the children to a clear floor area and show them the bricks. Tell them that you have a special job for them to do today. Can they please make you as many bridges as they can so that your car (or train) can test them out? Make sure they understand what a 'bridge' is, and show how your car can go *under* the bridge and also *over* it. Leave them while they work out how they can make as many bridges as possible with the bricks. Return to encourage them and also to try the bridges out, passing your car over and under. Now supply a selection of cars and trains for the children to develop their game. You can also provide a selection of larger-scale materials and challenge the children to make as large a bridge as possible.
Note	Observe each child selecting and experimenting with the construction materials – photography is a useful way to record this.
Things to say	• Is it *strong* enough for the train to go *over* it? • Is it *high* enough for the car to go *under* it? • Let's see whether it is *stable*.
Comments	

Knowledge and Understanding of the World

Knowledge and Understanding of the World
Designing and Making (40 – 60+ months)

Development matters	Play and practical support
Construct with a purpose in mind, using a variety of resources.	When the children have a definite plan in mind, encourage them to use you as a resource – not to make things for them, but to make suggestions of what materials and methods to try for themselves.

Sample activity	Rain Drain
What you need	A wide selection of craft materials and containers; yoghurt pots, cans, bottles, boxes, funnels, dishes. A permanent marker pen for yourself. A measuring cylinder. A tray.
How to prepare	Wait for a rainy day!
What to do	Gather some of the children together and invite them to invent a machine to catch the rain. Suggest they experiment today so that they can find the best designs. What do they think they would use? Support them as each decides what they are going to make and how to make it. At this stage, allow them to learn by trial and error – cardboard boxes are fine! Allow each child to make several if they wish to – this might all be part of their own 'experimenting'. Use name labels or descriptions so that you can remember whose is whose. When they are all ready, place them out in the rain on a tray. Later, bring them in and talk about which machines worked best. Perhaps the plastic cups have toppled over, or the cardboard boxes become soggy and lost their water. Show the children how you can use a measuring cylinder to find out which 'machine' has caught the most rain. Talk about what the children have learned and help them plan again. Repeat the activity next time it rains and complete your 'experiment'. You can also set up a weather station to measure rainfall, wind speed and air temperature and help the children find ways of recording their findings.
Note	Keep a photographic record of the children's constructions and what they said about them.
Things to say	• Which of these do you think should catch the most rain? • How could we make this one work better? • What do you think might have gone wrong here?
Comments	

Knowledge and Understanding of the World

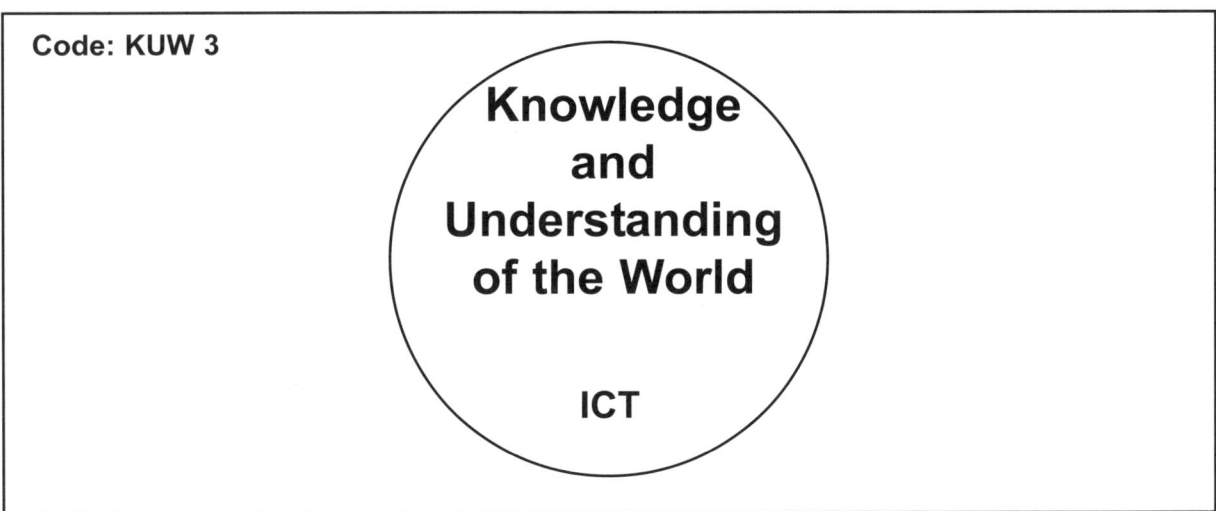

Code: KUW 3

Knowledge
and
Understanding
of the World

ICT

Development Matters

30 – 50 months
- Know how to operate simple equipment.

40 – 60+ months
- Complete a simple program on a computer.
- Use ICT to perform simple functions, such as selecting a channel on the TV remote control.
- Use a mouse and keyboard to interact with age-appropriate computer software.
- **Find out about and identify the uses of everyday technology and use information and communication technology and programmable toys to support their learning.**

You will find suggestions for *Look, listen and note*, *Effective practice* and *Planning and resourcing* in the EYFS Practice Guidance.

Knowledge and Understanding of the World

Knowledge and Understanding of the World
ICT (30 – 50 months)

Development matters	Play and practical support
Know how to operate simple equipment.	Digital cameras are useful on so many fronts – especially for involving the children in showing you what is important to them and also in recording their activities and evidence of learning and development.

Sample activity	**Look what *I* did!**
What you need	A simple digital camera that can easily be operated by the children with minimal support.
How to prepare	Label a wallet file (or engage the children in making their own portfolios) to keep their photographs in.
What to do	Discuss with your colleagues how you can involve the children more in your ongoing monitoring. For example, you could ask children what they feel pleased with and encourage them to photograph it for their own records. This might involve their taking a photograph of something they made. It might involve their asking one of you to take a photograph of what they are doing. Wherever possible, help the children operate the camera themselves and also involve them in the printing off and final selection.
Note	'Go with the child' and record what they wish you to, later gathering the photographs for the child's portfolio and adding a few words from the child to explain why that photograph was chosen.
Things to say	• What do you want me to photograph? • What was happening in this photograph? • Tell me why you wanted to keep *this* one. • What do you like about *this* photograph?
Comments	

Knowledge and Understanding of the World

Knowledge and Understanding of the World
ICT (40 – 60+ months)

Development matters	Play and practical support
Use ICT to perform simple functions, such as selecting a channel on the TV remote.	Try to involve the children themselves in many of the simple ICT tasks that you regularly carry out – such as downloading files, printing off or running a PowerPoint presentation.

Sample activity	Registration Time
What you need	Your usual PC, monitor, keyboard and mouse.
How to prepare	Design (or seek help from a IT-literate colleague) a simple self-registration system. Try to set up a simple sheet that can be scrolled down to show different children's faces, their names and a space to click to record that the child is present.
What to do	Plan an 'IT Week' with the children. As one way of 'doing things differently' that week, suggest that the children find their names on the computer and click to say that they are here. Have one of the helpers near to the computer to help if needs be. With a bit of expertise, you could develop this idea for all kinds of purposes – perhaps asking the children to record which activities they have tried out that session and which they 'rated' best.
Note	Note each child's interest and confidence when using the mouse and record how much support they still require.
Things to say	• Can you find yourself? • Try *scrolling* . . . now *click*. • Who else can you find here? • Who will you play with first, do you think?
Comments	

Knowledge and Understanding of the World

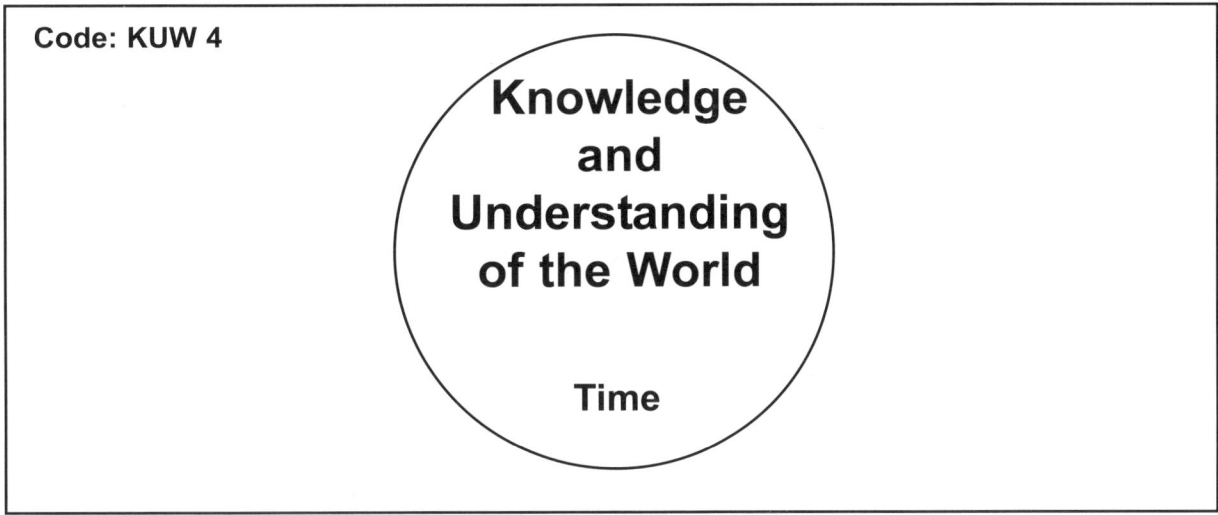

Code: KUW 4

Knowledge and Understanding of the World

Time

Development Matters

30 – 50 months

- Remember and talk about significant events in their own experience.
- Show interest in the lives of people familiar to them.
- Talk about past and future events.
- Develop an understanding of growth, decay and changes over time.

40 – 60+ months

- Begin to differentiate between past and present.
- Use time-related words in conversation.
- Understand about the seasons of the year and their regularity.
- Make short-term future plans.
- **Find out about past and present events in their own lives, and in those of their families and other people they know.**

You will find suggestions for *Look, listen and note*, *Effective practice* and *Planning and resourcing* in the EYFS Practice Guidance.

Knowledge and Understanding of the World

Knowledge and Understanding of the World
Time (30 – 50 months)

Development matters	Play and practical support
Talk about past and future events.	Spend a while talking with each child individually each session about what they would like to do today and, later, what they have been up to and how it went.

Sample activity	This is Me
What you need	Two or three photographs brought in from each child's home, showing them at different stages of their life. A photograph album with self-adhesive (removable) pages (or make your own from wallet files in a ring-binder). Small pieces of paper and a pen.
How to prepare	Tell parents that you will be doing a project 'All About Me' in your setting and can they help their child choose two or three photographs showing them as babies and toddlers, or on particular occasions or holidays. Ask parents to write the child's name on the back and a few words about the photograph. Assure them that they will have the photographs back afterwards and that you will look after them. With permission, scan any precious photographs so that you have your own copy to use. Because not every child will be able to bring in photographs, make sure you have a stock of your own which you have taken of the children over the previous months.
What to do	Sit down with individual children to share their photographs and mount them in your album, so that each child has a section of a page or two. Ask the children what they would like you to write on a small piece of paper to serve as a caption for each photograph. When you have photographs from three or four children, sit down as a group and share the photographs. Encourage them to talk about the past, the present and the future. Continue with your album until you have a section for everybody. Use the album as a talking point to encourage the children to talk about their past and future experiences. Encourage the children to imagine themselves as six year-olds, as eleven year-olds or even as grown-ups!
Note	Write down samples of the child's language concerning past and future events.
Things to say	• If they find tenses difficult ('I used to live', 'I lived', 'I live', 'I will live') then gently repeat back to them correctly what they are trying to say. • What were you doing in this picture? • What do you think you will play with when you are ten?
Comments	

Knowledge and Understanding of the World

Knowledge and Understanding of the World
Time (40 – 60+ months)

Development matters	Play and practical support
Make short-term future plans.	Adopting a 'plan-do-review' format can help children engage with their own planning and evaluate what they got out of each activity.

Sample activity	What next?
What you need	A felt board and Velcro tabs, or a white board and Blu-tak. Sheets of A5 paper and felt-tip pens.
How to prepare	No other preparation is needed.
What to do	Sit down with a group of the children and talk about their typical session. Ask them to tell you all the things they do in your group. Then take one idea at a time and draw a simple representation of this onto a sheet of paper; for example, a water tray, a paint pot or a teddy in a bed. Spread the cards out in front of you. Have you missed anything out? Make sure you have a picture for any 'link' times such as group time, drinks time and saying 'goodbye'. Now use the Blu-tak or Velcro tabs to arrange a few of these in a sequence onto a board, making a visual timetable for the children. Encourage them to refer to it from time to time between activities. Use it as a springboard to talk about the past, the present and the future. Children who have difficulties on the autistic spectrum or behavioural, social and emotional difficulties find 'visual timetables' particularly useful since it is reassuring for them to know at all times what will happen next.
Note	Observe whether a child can (a) plan an activity ahead, and (b) actually follow it through.
Things to say	• What did you do before story time? • What will you do next? • What would you like to try tomorrow?
Comments	

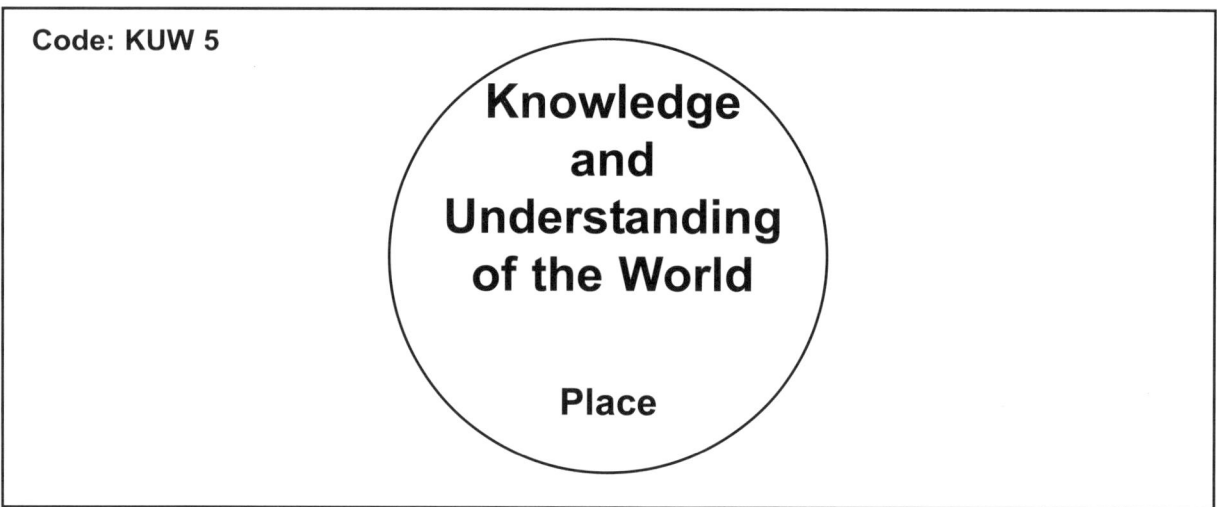

Code: KUW 5

Knowledge and Understanding of the World

Place

Development Matters

30 – 50 months
- Show an interest in the world in which they live.
- Comment and ask questions about where they live and the natural world.

40 – 60+ months
- Notice differences between features of the local environment.
- **Observe, find out about and identify features in the place they live and the natural world.**
- **Find out about their environment, and talk about those features they like and dislike.**

You will find suggestions for *Look, listen and note*, *Effective practice* and *Planning and resourcing* in the EYFS Practice Guidance.

Knowledge and Understanding of the World

Knowledge and Understanding of the World
Place (30 – 50 months)

Development matters	Play and practical support
Comment and ask questions about where they live and the natural world.	Forming positive relationships with parents and carers allows you to tune into the child's most meaningful experiences – their families and their homes.

Sample activity	My Home
What you need	Old wallpaper, sample books or off-cuts plus other collage materials, glue and sticking tools. The wherewithal to mount a 'street of houses' as a display on your wall.
How to prepare	Arrange all your collage materials on a table.
What to do	Talk with some of the children about their homes. During the discussion you are bound to have examples of many different living arrangements – houses, flats, bungalows, hostels, homes with a mum and a dad, homes with a grandma, homes with a mum and a sister, homes with more than one family and so on. Talk about this diversity. Suggest that you build a 'street' of their homes and show them your display space. Then encourage the children to cut out their own house from the wallpaper and add other collage material to make doors, windows and any other features they would like to add. Encourage them to draw in those who live in their home, perhaps looking out the window. Add the child's own words to your display to describe their home.
Note	How easily can each child talk about their home? Can they describe who lives there and describe it simply? Do they know any details of their address yet?
Things to say	• Who lives in your house? Can you draw them in? • Is it a house or a flat? • Do you know where you live? • Which one is your bedroom? • Do you have any pets?
Comments	

Knowledge and Understanding of the World

Knowledge and Understanding of the World
Place (40 – 60+ months)

Development matters	Play and practical support
Find out about their environment, and talk about those features they like and dislike.	Display photographs of the local environment including shops, places of worship and community/leisure centres.

Sample activity	Shopping Spree
What you need	A selection of coins: 1p and 2p or pretend money. A shopping corner with packaging, price labels, 1p and 2p coins. Perhaps a cash register, pretend 'scanner', bags and supermarket baskets.
How to prepare	Set up a shop/supermarket area for the children to play a buying and selling game. Mark the items with 1p or 2p.
What to do	Introduce the activity by talking about the shops in your local area. Give the children real 1p and 2p coins or pretend money to play with. Make sure all the helpers visit the shop regularly. Ask for art pictures for your walls as well as the usual shop items so that the children can arrange for someone to make these for you – outsourcing to friends perhaps! Follow this with a session with all the children planning a coming school fete or fund-raising event.
Note	Engage the children in talking about what shops they would like to see in their local community. Record sample answers.
Things to say	• Where do people go to buy food for their family? • What do you need to buy food? • Which shops do you go to? • What can you buy there? • Which do you like going to best?
Comments	

Knowledge and Understanding of the World

Code: KUW 6

Knowledge and Understanding of the World

Communities

Development Matters

30 – 50 months
- Express feelings about a significant personal event.
- Describe significant events for family or friends.
- Enjoy imaginative and role-play with peers.
- Show interest in different occupations and ways of life.

40 – 60+ months
- Gain an awareness of the cultures and beliefs of others.
- Feel a sense of belonging to own community and place.
- **Begin to know about their own cultures and beliefs and those of other people.**

You will find suggestions for *Look, listen and note*, *Effective practice* and *Planning and resourcing* in the EYFS Practice Guidance.

Knowledge and Understanding of the World

Knowledge and Understanding of the World
Communities (30 – 50 months)

Development matters	Play and practical support
Show interest in different occupations and ways of life.	You can arrange all kinds of themed areas to encourage the children to focus on different ways of life. You might find the activity 'At the Vets' on page 28 helpful as well.

Sample activity	Hairdressing Salon
What you need	Props for a hairdressing corner. Very soft brushes and large combs, towels, foam rollers perhaps, safe mirrors, 'pretend' wash bowls, hair scrunchies, bands, clips, ornaments.
How to prepare	Set up your props and resources to suggest a hairdressing corner – make sure that it is unisex!
What to do	Move into the hairdressing corner to start the game rolling. Be prepared to sit back for a while as you are groomed and decorated! Encourage all the children to visit your unisex hair salon or to take a turn at being a hairdresser. Admire yourselves in the mirror. Talk about the children's own experiences of seeing hairdressers and develop the game with further props and ideas as the children think of them. Help the children think of the sequences involved; first the hair is combed, then washed, then dried, then styled. Lead up to a grand fashion parade at the end of the session. Follow up by painting pictures of amazing hairstyles or modelling them in play dough.
Note	Note which children were interested and became involved with this activity and provide an example of how each engaged with it.
Things to say	• What will I look like? • What happens next? • Have you been to a hairdresser's shop? • Are you enjoying being a hairdresser?
Comments	

Knowledge and Understanding of the World

Knowledge and Understanding of the World
Communities (40 – 60+ months)

Development matters	Play and practical support
Feel a sense of belonging to own community and place.	Start by planning some activities that include everyone and encourage a sense of belonging to and identity with the group itself.

Sample activity	Friends and Neighbours
What you need	Sheets of coloured paper in the outline of a house, paints, brushes, mounting paper, scissors and a staple gun for yourself.
How to prepare	Introduce the activity when you are sitting all together during circle time.
What to do	Ask the children if they know what a 'neighbour' is. Find out as you talk together which children live near to each other and who lives in different neighbourhoods or villages of your area. Explain that you will be making a large frieze showing where everyone lives and who their neighbours are. In groups of three to four, invite the children to select house-shaped paper and paints and paint a picture of their families and then their neighbours in different houses. As they work, talk together about friends and neighbours. When the paintings are dry, ask for the children's help as you mount them on the wall, adding your own landmarks to make a frieze of your community, village or area of town. Take the opportunity to talk about 'friendly' behaviour.
Note	Record examples that show you that a child has a sense of belonging to your group and also to a particular neighbourhood, community or faith.
Things to say	• Do you have a friend who lives near to you? • Do you know who your neighbours are? • Who has children living next door to them? • How do you know when someone is your friend? • How do you become a 'good' neighbour?
Comments	

Knowledge and Understanding of the World

Area of Learning: Knowledge and Understanding of the World		
Focus:	Age Range:	Code: KUW _____
Development matters		Play and practical support

Sample activity	
What you need	
How to prepare	
What to do	
Note	
Things to say	
Comments	

Ⓟ

Completed by: **Date:**

Knowledge and Understanding of the World
(30–60+ months)

Date of activity:	Supervised by:

Children involved:

Comments

Date of activity:	Supervised by:

Children involved:

Comments

Date of activity:	Supervised by:

Children involved:

Comments

Ⓟ

Physical Development

(30–60+ months)

Physical Development
(30–60+ months)

Section index

Sample Activities

	30 – 50 months	40 – 60+ months
PD 1 Movement and Space	Page 104	Page 105
PD 2 Health and Bodily Awareness	Page 107	Page 108
PD 3 Using Equipment and Materials	Page 110	Page 111

A blank planner for you to copy and complete for the children is on page 112. There are also non-specific blank planners for you to copy and complete at the back of the book. There is a monitoring sheet for you to use and adapt on page 113.

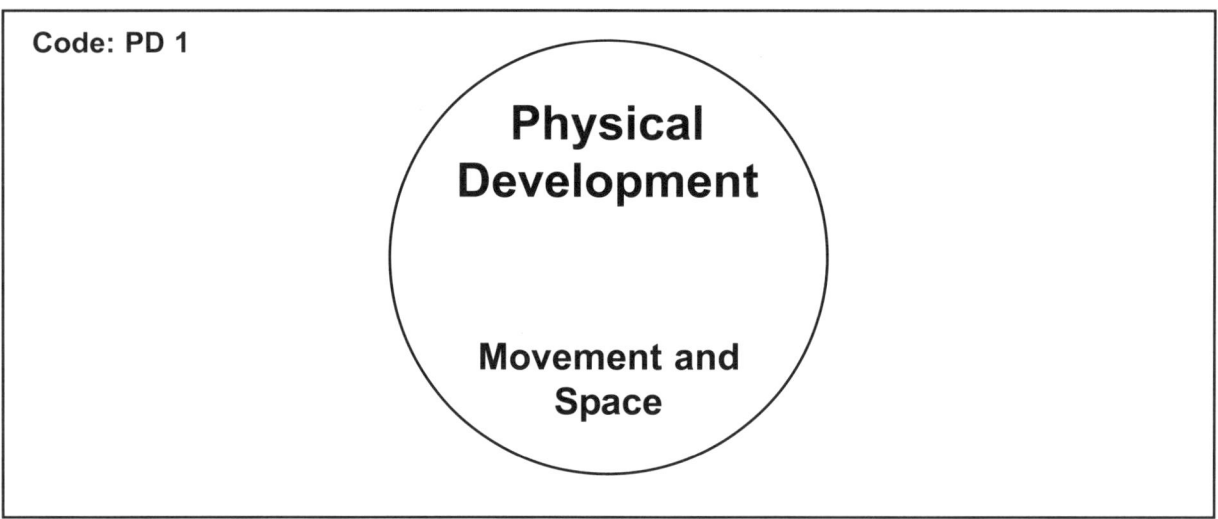

Code: PD 1

Physical Development

Movement and Space

Development Matters

30 – 50 months

- Move freely with pleasure and confidence in a range of ways, such as slithering, shuffling, rolling, crawling, walking, running, jumping, skipping, sliding and hopping.
- Use movement to express feelings.
- Negotiate space successfully when playing racing and chasing games with other children, adjusting speed or changing direction to avoid obstacles.
- Sit up, stand up and balance on various parts of the body.
- Demonstrate the control necessary to hold a shape or fixed position.
- Operate equipment by means of pushing and pulling movements.
- Mount stairs, steps or climbing equipment using alternate feet.
- Negotiate an appropriate pathway when walking, running or using a wheelchair or other mobility aids, both indoors and outdoors.
- Judge body space in relation to spaces available when fitting into confined spaces or negotiating openings and boundaries.
- Show respect for other children's personal space when playing among them.
- Persevere in repeating some actions or attempts when developing a new skill.
- Collaborate in devising and sharing tasks, including those which involve accepting rules.

You will find suggestions for *Look, listen and note*, *Effective practice* and *Planning and resourcing* in the EYFS Practice Guidance.

Physical Development

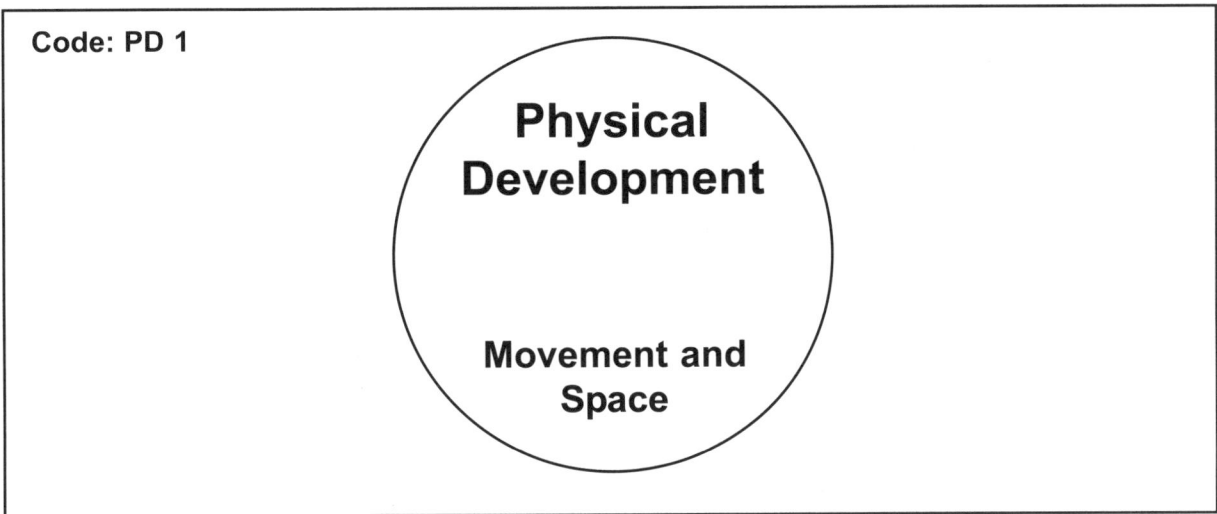

Code: PD 1

Physical Development

Movement and Space

Development Matters

40 – 60+ months

- Go backwards and sideways as well as forwards.
- Experiment with different ways of moving.
- Initiate new combinations of movement and gesture in order to express and respond to feelings, ideas and experiences.
- Jump off an object and land appropriately.
- Show understanding of the need for safety when tackling new challenges.
- Avoid dangerous places and equipment.
- Construct with large materials such as cartons, fabric and planks.
- **Move with confidence, imagination and in safety.**
- **Move with control and coordination.**
- **Travel around, under, over, and through balancing and climbing equipment.**
- **Show awareness of space, of themselves and of others.**

You will find suggestions for *Look, listen and note*, *Effective practice* and *Planning and resourcing* in the EYFS Practice Guidance.

Physical Development

Physical Development
Movement and Space (30 – 50 months)

Development matters	Play and practical support
Demonstrate the control necessary to hold a shape or fixed position.	Choose a special group signal to use when you really need everyone to stop what they are doing and stay still – do not over use!

Sample activity	The Scarecrow Game
What you need	A selection of scarecrows' hats, gloves and jackets for yourselves – try the local charity shops. Also some black, draping clothes for one of your helpers to become the crow! A tambourine or drum.
How to prepare	Place your scarecrow clothes and any props into a large box.
What to do	Invite a few children to join you and explore your scarecrow paraphernalia. Talk about scarecrows and what they are for, perhaps sharing some pictures together and singing 'I'm a dingle dangle scarecrow'. Spend some time dressing yourselves up as scarecrows and move to an open space, indoors or out. Now play a game with the crow – as soon as the crow appears the scarecrows should waggle their arms in the wind and frighten it away! As soon as it flies away, beat the tambourine as a signal for them to freeze absolutely still. Once familiar with the game, some of the children will love to take a turn at being the crow – or even a flock of hungry crows!
Note	Watch whether each child can hold a fixed position – you might even challenge some to try doing so on one leg or in unusual positions.
Things to say	• Here comes the crow again – frighten it away! • Get ready to . . . FREEZE! • Who can make a really scary shape? Now FREEZE!
Comments	

Physical Development

Physical Development
Movement and Space (40 – 60+ months)

Code: PD 1

Development matters	Play and practical support
Go backwards and sideways as well as forwards.	Creating simple obstacle courses provides children with natural opportunities to move in all directions and enjoy themselves at the same time.

Sample activity	Anything You Can Do
What you need	You will need chalk, hoops, bean bags, some big cardboard boxes, and any other items you can devise for a simple obstacle course.
How to prepare	Set up your obstacle course in advance – chalk squares to jump between, hoops to pass over your heads, bean bags to toss or to carry, chalk snakes to run along, cardboard boxes to climb through and so on. This is a good activity for the outdoors if you have a suitable space.
What to do	Invite a small group of children to join your game of 'follow my leader'. All they have to do is follow you along the course, doing what the person in front does. Make small variations the second time through, so that they follow different actions with the obstacles. Now stand back and allow any of the children who wish to make their own course, and set up their own following games. Be there to help them if they ask you to. Help the children find more interesting materials and apparatus to add to their own game.
Note	Observe the range of movements each child makes - how they can balance, crawl, climb, move sideways, stoop and step backwards.
Things to say	• What would happen if we all tried to go through the obstacle course at the same time? • Are you stuck – how are you going to come out again? • Can anyone show me how you crawl *under*?
Comments	

Physical Development

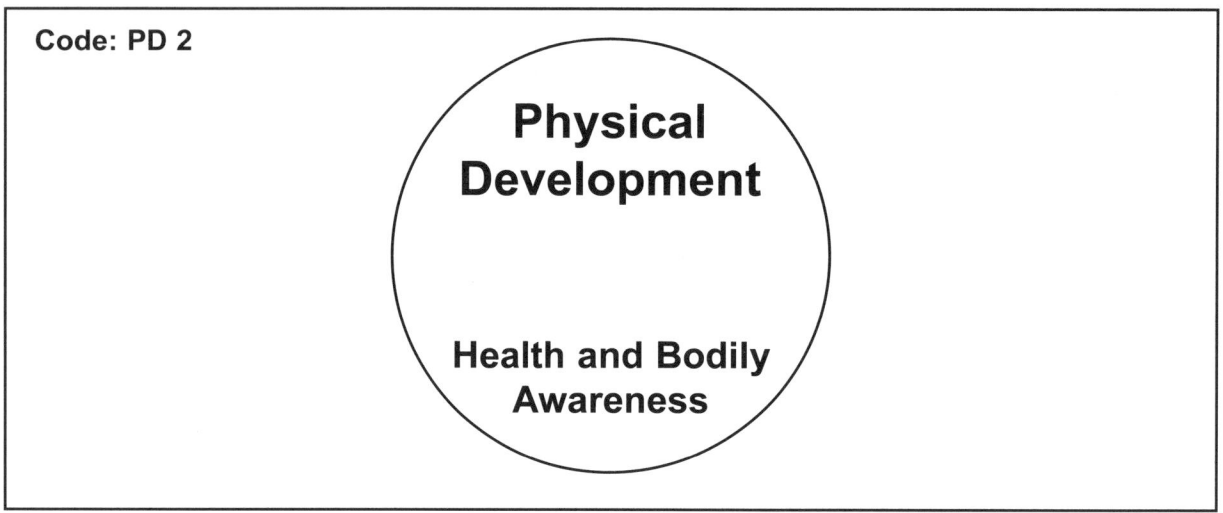

Code: PD 2

Physical Development

Health and Bodily Awareness

Development Matters

30 – 50 months

- Show awareness of own needs with regard to eating, sleeping and hygiene.
- Often need adult support to meet those needs.
- Show awareness of a range of healthy practices with regard to eating, sleeping and hygiene.
- Observe the effects of activity on their bodies.

40 – 60+ months

- Show some understanding that good practices with regard to exercise, eating, sleeping and hygiene can contribute to good health.
- **Recognise the importance of keeping healthy, and those things which contribute to this.**
- **Recognise the changes that happen to their bodies when they are active.**

You will find suggestions for *Look, listen and note, Effective practice* and *Planning and resourcing* in the EYFS Practice Guidance.

Physical Development

Physical Development
Health and Bodily Awareness (30 – 50 months)

Development matters	Play and practical support
Show awareness of own needs with regard to eating, sleeping and hygiene.	Children of this age still need to pace themselves – make sure you have areas for being quiet and restful as well as busy and active.

Sample activity	Food Fun
What you need	A selection of natural and fresh foods from many cultures to taste and enjoy. You might select wholemeal bread and butter, unprocessed cheese, natural yoghurt with honey, fresh fruit, raw vegetables, couscous, home-made savoury rice (etc.) Plates, spoons, kitchen knife (for yourself), clingfilm. A selection of packaging from highly processed foods such as a cola bottle, dry noodle dishes, sweets and lollipops, sweet biscuits.
How to prepare	Prepare the food in advance, cutting it into bite size portions or arranging in serving bowls and covering. Make sure that you are aware of any allergies before planning this activity.
What to do	Gather some of the children together and talk about what they like to eat. Which foods are really good for you? Talk about fruits and vegetables for staying healthy – milk, cheese and yoghurts for helping you grow strong. Ask them which foods they like. The children are bound to mention sweets, crisps, biscuits. Use some of your packaging to prompt replies. Ask them whether food that they like is always good for them. Let the children work this out with their own ideas. Then suggest that the children taste some foods which are really good for them and see if they also taste good. Enjoy your tasting session together. Encourage children to sort pictures and packages of healthy food from food which is not so good for you. Children who are allergic to certain food might welcome the chance to talk about this with the other children.
Note	Note how aware the children are of eating healthily and retain photographs of them selecting their favourite foods.
Things to say	• Which foods do you really like? • Are the foods that you like always good for you?
Comments	

Physical Development

Physical Development
Health and Bodily Awareness (40 – 60+ months)

Development matters	Play and practical support
Recognise the importance of keeping healthy, and those things which contribute to this.	Introduce the idea that activity and exercise are good for you and help to keep you fit and healthy. Look for natural opportunities to raise this and to encourage the children.

Sample activity	Bend and Stretch
What you need	An open space to move in. CD or tape of rhythmical music and player.
How to prepare	No other preparation is needed.
What to do	Invite a small group of children to join you for an exercise 'circuit'. Encourage them to watch you carefully and try to copy everything you do. Stand in front of them and begin to do these exercises, pretending to be in training (for the next Olympics?). Keep it fun and not too energetic. Practise each exercise five times. Count slowly: 1–2–3–4 as you make each movement, counting one number for each bar of the music. The idea is to move and stretch slowly and in a controlled way, rather than to move jerkily and quickly. • Move your neck slowly to one side and then to the other. • Move your neck to look slowly down at your feet then up in the air. • Move your head slowly round in a circular movement. • Repeat in the other direction. • Stretch hands up in the air with fingers reaching up, then lower to your side. • Keep hands straight and stretch them round to one side at tummy level, reaching behind you. Repeat the other side. • Keep arms straight and reach down to your toes, moving them in a gentle circle to the sides, straightening up as you stretch them above your head. Repeat for the other direction. These are gentle exercises and should be fun for everyone, whatever their shape or size.
Note	Observe whether children find movement and physical activity intrinsically enjoyable and whether they realise that this is good for their health.
Things to say	• What does that exercise feel like? • Why do people exercise? • What do you think *this* exercise is good for?
Comments	

Physical Development

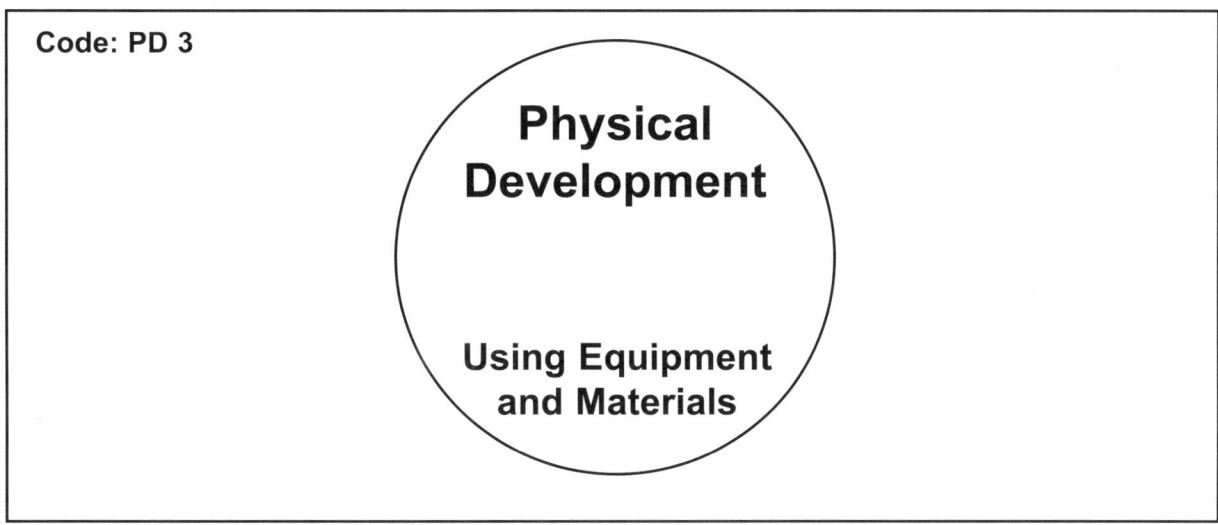

Code: PD 3

Physical Development

Using Equipment and Materials

Development Matters

30 – 50 months

- Engage in activities requiring hand-eye coordination.
- Use one-handed tools and equipment.
- Show increasing control over clothing and fastenings.
- Show increasing control in using equipment for climbing, scrambling, sliding and swinging.
- Demonstrate increasing skill and control in the use of mark-making implements, blocks, construction sets and small-world activities.
- Understand that equipment and tools have to be used safely.

40 – 60+ months

- Explore malleable materials by patting, stroking, squeezing, pinching and twisting them.
- Use increasing control over an object, such as a ball, by touching, pushing, patting, throwing, catching or kicking it.
- Manipulate materials to achieve a planned effect.
- Use simple tools to effect changes to the materials.
- Show understanding of how to transport and store equipment safely.
- Practise some appropriate safety measures without direct supervision.
- **Use a range of small and large equipment.**
- **Handle tools, objects, construction and malleable materials safely and with increasing control.**

You will find suggestions for *Look, listen and note*, *Effective practice* and *Planning and resourcing* in the EYFS Practice Guidance.

Physical Development

Physical Development
Using Equipment and Materials (30 – 50 months)

Development matters	Play and practical support
Show increasing control over clothing and fastenings.	Use your knowledge of each child's stage to offer just the right amount of help and no more, always encouraging their efforts.

Sample activity	Changing Rooms
What you need	An augmented dressing up selection (clothes, hats, scarves, shoes, gloves etc.) and a standard mirror which is safe for the children. If possible, shelves and low rails.
How to prepare	Arrange the clothing on low rails and on shelves (you can improvise using cardboard boxes on their sides) to look like a department store. Spread the clothes out so that they can be easily seen and are attractive. Set up the mirror where children can admire themselves.
What to do	Play alongside the children to start this game going. Imagine you are shopping in a department store and buying new clothes. Be on hand to help the children put on the clothes and to help with fastenings, using this as a natural opportunity for showing them how to manage themselves. This is an ideal opportunity to teach dressing and undressing skills. You might also provide a manikin (or one of the helpers!) for children to 'design' whole outfits. Stand back as the game develops and step in if the children need help with fastening or unfastening. End with fashion parade for any of the other children to come and watch.
Note	Note whether a child can do up/undo buttons, zips and other fastenings. Can they do so independently when arriving and leaving the group?
Things to say	• Can you find the button holes? • Can you do my big buttons up please? • Where does the zip foot go?
Comments	

Physical Development

Physical Development
Using Equipment and Materials (40 – 60+ months)

Development matters	Play and practical support
Use increasing control over an object, such as a ball, by touching, pushing, patting, throwing, catching or kicking it.	Provide a wide range of balls in your play area – and also slower moving objects for catching and throwing (such as beanbags, balloons and bubbles).

Sample activity	On the Ball
What you need	A selection of balls including a large beach ball, a tennis ball, a small rubber ball and a lightweight plastic ball.
How to prepare	Encourage some of the children to sit in a circle on a mat, indoors or out.
What to do	Tell the children you are going to play a copying game with some of the balls. First, invite them to pass the large beach ball gently around the circle, passing it from hands to hands. Then challenge them to throw it very gently and quietly to their neighbour so that it travels all around the circle without falling to the floor. When the children are managing this, try with a smaller ball, varying the size of the circle or the space between certain children to make this easier. Then try a 'copycat' game with each child taking a turn in throwing, rolling, tossing up and catching or bouncing the ball with the others taking a turn to copy afterward as the ball is again passed across the circle. Once you have established which children need more support, play with them in a smaller group, choosing the best ball to make the activity enjoyable and successful.
Note	Keep a note of the stage each child has reached in touching, pushing, patting, throwing, catching or kicking the different sized balls.
Things to say	• Take a look through your selection of balls. Which balls do the children think would be easiest to pass/kick/throw/catch etc.? Try them and see. • What do we mean by passing the ball 'gently' to each other?
Comments	

Physical Development

Area of Learning: Physical Development		
Focus:	**Age Range:**	**Code: PD _____**
Development matters		**Play and practical support**

Sample activity	
What you need	
How to prepare	
What to do	
Note	
Things to say	
Comments	

Ⓟ

Completed by: **Date:**

Physical Development
(30–60+ months)

Date of activity:	Supervised by:

Children involved:

Comments

Date of activity:	Supervised by:

Children involved:

Comments

Date of activity:	Supervised by:

Children involved:

Comments

Ⓟ

Creative Development

(30–60+ months)

Creative Development
(30–60+ months)

Section index

Sample Activities

<table>
<tr><td></td><td></td><td>30 – 50
months</td><td>40 – 60+
months</td></tr>
<tr><td>CD 1</td><td>Being Creative – Responding to Experiences, Expressing and Communicating Ideas</td><td>Page 117</td><td>Page 118</td></tr>
<tr><td>CD 2</td><td>Exploring Media and Materials</td><td>Page 120</td><td>Page 121</td></tr>
<tr><td>CD 3</td><td>Creating Music and Dance</td><td>Page 123</td><td>Page 124</td></tr>
<tr><td>CD 4</td><td>Developing Imagination and Imaginative Play</td><td>Page 126</td><td>Page 127</td></tr>
</table>

A blank planner for you to copy and complete for the children is on page 128. There are also non-specific blank planners for you to copy and complete at the back of the book. There is a monitoring sheet for you to use and adapt on page 129.

Code: CD 1

Creative Development

**Being Creative –
Responding to
Experiences, Expressing
and Communicating
Ideas**

Development Matters

30 – 50 months

- Use language and other forms of communication to share the things they create, or to indicate personal satisfaction or frustration.
- Explore and experience using a range of senses and movement.
- Capture experiences and responses with music, dance, paint and other materials or words.
- Develop preferences for forms of expression.

40 – 60+ months

- Talk about personal intentions, describing what they are trying to do.
- Respond to comments and questions, entering into dialogue about their creations.
- Make comparisons and create new connections.
- **Respond in a variety of ways to what they see, hear, smell, touch and feel.**
- **Express and communicate their ideas, thoughts and feelings by using a widening range of materials, suitable tools, imaginative and role-play, movement, designing and making, and a variety of songs and musical instruments.**

You will find suggestions for *Look, listen and note*, *Effective practice* and *Planning and resourcing* in the EYFS Practice Guidance.

Creative Development

Creative Development
Being Creative – Responding to Experiences ... (30 – 50 months)   Code: CD 1

Development matters	Play and practical support
Develop preferences for forms of expression.	You can introduce children to a wide range of media by planning 'taster' activities and then providing a wide range of resources for them to create and explore further.

Sample activity	Artistic Me
What you need	A selection of stickers – a different type for each activity on offer (see below) plus a planned music activity, dance activity, craft activity and painting activity. You can add more depending on your resources and ideas. A digital camera.
How to prepare	Set up the various activities on offer and arrange for a helper to lead each one.
What to do	When the children first arrive and meet together for Group Time, tell them that you have some special activities for them today. Go through what they are and show examples of the kinds of things that the children will be doing. Then explain that the idea is that everybody should try each activity on offer and that they will receive a different sticker for each one they try. So if they have a go at *everything*, they will end up with five (or however many) stickers on themselves! Some children might prefer using a little sticker book that you made together and sharing it with parents and carers later. Keep plenty of photographs to talk about later so that you can talk about what the children enjoyed best.
Note	Note down what the children say about their different activities and which they liked best. You can also use the photographs themselves as a record of achievement and involvement, perhaps adding comments that the child has made about each one.
Things to say	• What were you doing in this picture? • Which did you enjoy best and why?
Comments	

Creative Development

Creative Development
Being Creative – Responding to Experiences ... (40 – 60+ months)   Code: CD 1

Development matters	Play and practical support
Express and communicate their ideas, thoughts and feelings by using a widening range of materials, suitable tools, imaginative and role-play, movement, designing and making, and a variety of songs and musical instruments.	Plan structured activities to introduce a range of resources and media and then make sure a wide range of resources is readily available for the children to choose from. In this way, they will express their feelings in flexible imaginative ways.

Sample activity	Letting it Out
What you need	A CD player with a selection of music representing a wide range of feelings, tempos, genres, origins and styles. An open space and your usual range of art, craft, dressing up, mark-making and small, world play materials.
How to prepare	Set out your usual resources for creative play.
What to do	Move to an open space and tell a small group of children you are going to play some music to move and dance to. First, they must listen carefully and see how the music is telling them to move. Sit the children down as you play a short piece of music (no more than thirty seconds). Now encourage the children to move freely, joining in yourself. Describe the children's dancing and movement to them, and tell them how it is making you feel. Encourage at all stages. Continue the activity with three or four pieces of music, and then sit down for a rest. Which was each child's favourite? Talk about what the music makes you want to do – paint a picture perhaps, dress up like a pirate, make a seaside in the sand tray. Encourage each child to move onto another creative activity, building on what they have just heard and thought about. Later, you could encourage some of the children to use percussion and movement to illustrate a story, by giving to sound effects and a musical background.
Note	Look out for examples of the children transferring their thoughts and feelings from one media to another.
Things to say	• Does this music make you feel happy or sad, angry or calm? • Does it make you want to jump or to float smoothly? • Does it sound like a giant or a mouse (etc.)?
Comments	

Creative Development

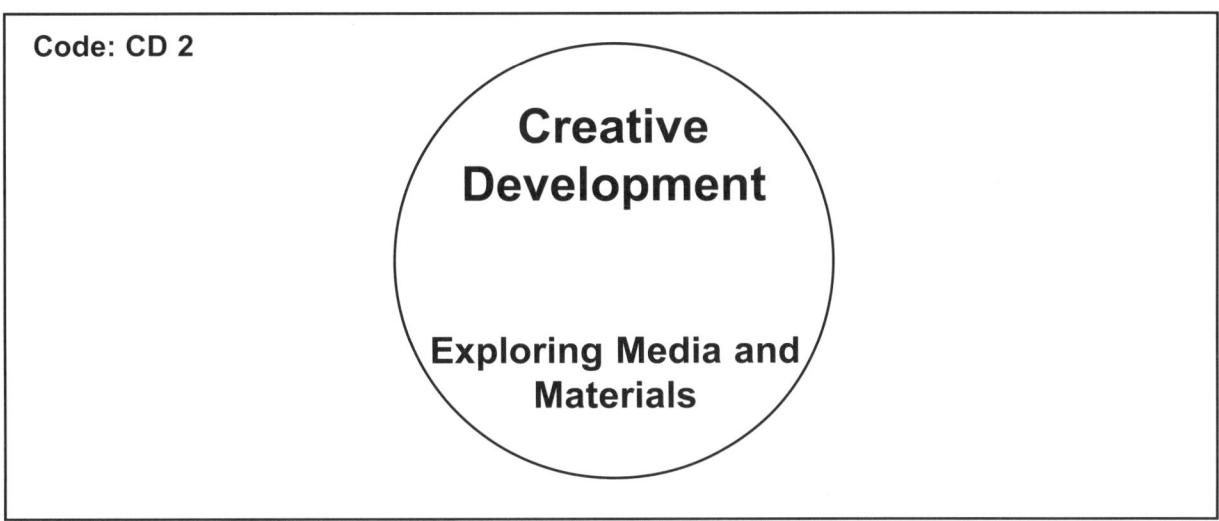

Code: CD 2

Creative Development

Exploring Media and Materials

Development Matters

30 – 50 months

- Begin to be interested in and describe the texture of things.
- Explore colour and begin to differentiate between colours.
- Differentiate marks and movements on paper.
- Use their bodies to explore texture and space.
- Understand that they can use lines to enclose a space, and then begin to use these shapes to represent objects.
- Create 3D structures.
- Begin to construct, stacking blocks vertically and horizontally, making enclosures and creating spaces.

40 – 60+ months

- Explore what happens when they mix colours.
- Choose particular colours to use for a purpose.
- Understand that different media can be combined to create new effects.
- Experiment to create different textures.
- Create constructions, collages, paintings and drawings.
- Use ideas involving fitting, overlapping, in, out, enclosure, grids and sun-like shapes.
- Work creatively on a large or small scale.
- **Explore colour, texture, shape, form and space in two or three dimensions.**

You will find suggestions for *Look, listen and note*, *Effective practice* and *Planning and resourcing* in the EYFS Practice Guidance.

Creative Development

Creative Development
Exploring Media and Materials (30 – 50 months)

Code: CD 2

Development matters	Play and practical support
Begin to construct, stacking blocks vertically and horizontally, making enclosures and creating spaces.	You can encourage construction play by starting large-scale with packaging and cardboard boxes, later refining down to smaller blocks.

Sample activity	Conveyer Belt
What you need	Large wooden bricks, a large box and a solid floor surface to build on.
How to prepare	Put all the bricks and tools in the large box and place it next to you.
What to do	Ask a small group of children to sit on the floor in a circle with you. Teach them this building song, sung to the tune of 'Here we go round the mulberry bush'.
	This is the way we build a wall, build a wall, build a wall *This is the way we build a wall, working all together!*
	Now get one brick at a time out of the box and show the children how to pass it from hand to hand around the circle. When the verse finishes, ask the child holding the brick to start building a wall. Sing the verse again as you pass bricks around the circle and the wall grows. Now try some new words:
	This is the way we build a tower (etc.)
	This time, pass the bricks round so that the child left with the brick at the end of the verse adds it to a tower. Your last verse is:
	This is the way we put up a fence (etc.)
	This time, extend your wall into an enclosure and end up by going off to find soft toy animals to graze inside it!
Note	Observe how the children carry over the skills of stacking and enclosing into their free imaginative play.
Things to say	• Can we balance another on top? • How big will our field be? • What animals do we need for our field?
Comments	

Creative Development

Creative Development
Exploring Media and Materials (40 – 60+ months)

Development matters	Play and practical support
Create constructions, collages, painting and drawings.	Collect attractive and unusual collage material in order to stimulate the children's imagination and creativity.

Sample activity	Rainbow Ribbons
What you need	Large sheets of paper, glue, a wide selection of collage and sticking materials such as pasta, straws, pulses, sequins, stars, foil, glitter sticks, small pieces of paper, feathers, paper doily, scraps of material and lace, coloured feathers. A plastic bowl for each child. Nursery scissors if asked for, broad ribbon or strips of crepe paper. A large tray.
How to prepare	Collect together the collage materials. Spread these out on a large tray so that children can see them clearly and turn them over gently.
What to do	Talk about all your materials and look through them together, admiring each piece. Then invite each child to select a few items for their bowl. Once all the pieces have been chosen, show how each can be glued onto a broad ribbon or strip of crepe paper to make a multi-coloured streamer. Stay close to help with the first few pieces, then leave them to work independently and to talk to and share with each other. Reinforce the stickings-on of the heavier pieces with a stapler if you need to, then hang the strips up where they will flutter and turn in the breeze. The important aspect of this activity is the choosing not the making – so if the child has other ideas of what to do with their pieces (such as treasure for the pirates' area) then that is excellent too!
Note	Observe how the child selects their collage pieces and note their reasons and choices.
Things to say	• Use describing words to introduce the shiny, lacy, feathery, hard things. • Talk about their colours and their textures. • Keep this a relaxed commentary rather than a list of questions.
Comments	

Creative Development

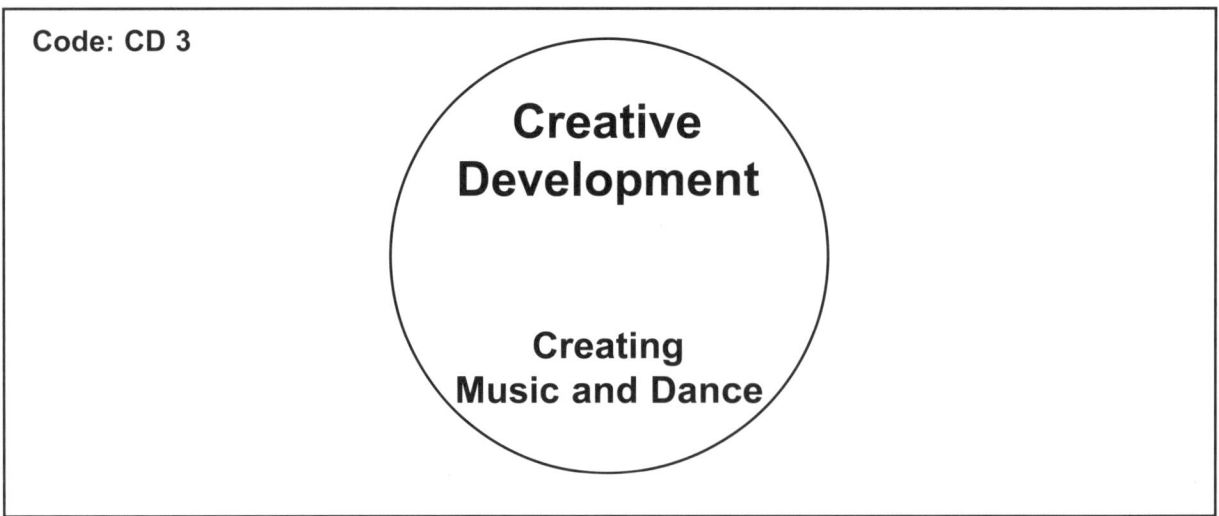

Code: CD 3

Creative Development

Creating Music and Dance

Development Matters

30 – 50 months
- Enjoy joining in with dancing and ring games.
- Sing a few familiar songs.
- Sing to themselves and make up simple songs.
- Tap out simple repeated rhythms and make some up.
- Explore and learn how sounds can be changed.
- Imitate and create movement in response to music.

40 – 60+ months
- Begin to build a repertoire of songs and dances.
- Explore the different sounds of instruments.
- Begin to move rhythmically.
- **Recognise and explore how sounds can be changed, sing simple songs from memory, recognise repeated sounds and sound patterns and match movements to music.**

You will find suggestions for *Look, listen and note*, *Effective practice* and *Planning and resourcing* in the EYFS Practice Guidance.

Creative Development

Creative Development
Creating Music and Dance (30 – 50 months)

Development matters	Play and practical support
Sing a few familiar songs.	You will find a wealth of ideas for using music and song to support children's learning and development in the EYFS in the book *Music Makers* (QEd Publications).

Sample activity	Three Wobbly Jellyfish
What you need	A large tambourine.
How to prepare	No other preparation is needed.
What to do	Sit on the floor in a circle with a small group of children. Tell the children that you are going to play some shaking music. When they hear it, they are to shake all over; shake their arms, shake their toes, shake their bodies all over. When it stops, they should stop too. Move round the circle as you shake the tambourine loudly, encouraging them to shake. Then beat the tambourine once loudly, stopping absolutely still. Praise children by name for looking and listening. Repeat three or four times, encouraging laughter and giggles as you shake, and scanning all the children's faces when you have stopped. Move on straight away to a shaking song. This one can be sung to the tune of 'Three Blind mice'. *Three green jellyfish, Three green jellyfish,* *Sat upon a rock, sat upon a rock,* *The first one felt like a swim, you know,* *And slithered away to the sea, you know,* *And left the rest on their own-i-o,* *Just two green jellyfish.* Wobble all over for the 'jellyfish'. Raise your hands in the air and wobble them down all the way to the sea for the 'slithering'. Repeat until there are no jellyfish left on the rock.
Note	Observe each child's response to music and song. Are they clearly showing enjoyment and are there any signs of anticipation and joining in?
Things to say	• Who's listening? • Who's looking? (Praise children for looking and listening so well.) • 'Perry, you *are* listening well' (etc.)?
Comments	

Creative Development

Creative Development
Creating Music and Dance (40 – 60+ months)

Development matters	Play and practical support
Begin to move rhythmically.	You will find plenty of ideas for helping children develop all kinds of learning skills through a regular music circle time in *Music Makers* (QEd Publications).

Sample activity	Taking the Lead
What you need	A selection of musical percussion instruments, a musical CD and player and a large portable drum. Make sure your CD collection represents a wide range of feelings, tempos, genres, origins and styles.
How to prepare	Clear a wide space, or move the activity tables away from the walls so that you can march in a procession around the room. In the warmer weather, prepare an outdoor area instead if you can be noisy and safe there.
What to do	Use this activity at the end of a longer music session. Invite each child to take turns choosing their own musical instrument. Explain that when *you* play, they can play too. When *you* stop, they must stop too. Have a few goes, playing a lively CD and leading with your own drum beats. Now invite individual children to take the lead, and everyone else must copy their starting and stopping. Give them the drum to play. Finally, let children take turns in leading the marchers round the room, starting and stopping, as you all march rhythmically to the beat. Finish by taking the lead (and the drum) once more and playing 'follow-my-leader' as you take up different rhythms and beats, all moving accordingly.
Note	The earliest rhythm that children can usually move to is a simple 'one-two' beat. Observe which children can manage this, especially if you emphasise it strongly. Older children will manage to vary their pace and rhythm with different CDs.
Things to say	• Who is listening? Who is looking? • Look at . . . marching! • How does this music make you want to move?
Comments	

Creative Development

Creative Development

Developing Imagination and Imaginative Play

Development Matters

30 – 50 months
- Notice what adults do, imitating what is observed and then doing it spontaneously when the adult is not there.
- Use available resources to create props to support role-play.
- Develop a repertoire of actions by putting a sequence of movements together.
- Engage in imaginative play and role-play based on own first-hand experiences.

40 – 60+ months
- Introduce a storyline or narrative into their play.
- Play alongside other children who are engaged in the same theme.
- Play cooperatively as part of a group to act out a narrative.
- **Use their imagination in art and design, music, dance, imaginative and role-play and stories.**

You will find suggestions for *Look, listen and note*, *Effective practice* and *Planning and resourcing* in the EYFS Practice Guidance.

Creative Development

Creative Development
Developing Imagination & Imaginative Play (30 – 50 months)

Development matters	Play and practical support
Use available resources to create props to support role-play.	When children are playing imaginatively, step in to make suggestions for props and resources to support their play, but know when to stand back and allow them to develop their own ideas too!

Sample activity	Three Wishes
What you need	A 'magic wand' (a glittery stick is ideal).
How to prepare	None at all.
What to do	This is an activity for group or circle time. Sit down with the children on a carpet. Tell them you are going to play a 'just pretend' game. You are going to pretend to be a magician and make all the children's wishes come true. Ask all the children to think very hard what they would like to wish for, but not to tell you yet. Start with a confident child, and ask for their wish. Pretend to wave a magic wand and pretend that the wish has been granted. Encourage all the children to join the make believe, perhaps pretending to go on holiday, or sitting down to a birthday party. Encourage the children to look for suitable props to support the idea. Let each child have a turn at making a wish, perhaps over several sessions. Use your role playing to involve the children's imagination and to develop their resourcefulness in searching for props. After the activity, use your dressing-up materials and other props to encourage further imaginative play. For older children you might make the wish more detailed. For example: 'Imagine you are waking up one morning. What would be your very best sort of day?'
Note	Observe the follow-up play and note examples of each child looking for or using props to support their imaginative play.
Things to say	• How would you like us to dress for your party? • What would you like to be in your birthday presents (etc.)? • What can we use for candles?
Comments	

Creative Development

Creative Development
Developing Imagination & Imaginative Play (40 – 60+ months)   Code: CD 4

Development matters	Play and practical support
Introduce a storyline or narrative into their play.	Once you have all shared a particularly motivating story, rhyme or activity together, make sure that you have put out resources and props that would naturally contribute towards any follow-up play that may have been inspired.

Sample activity	Train Game
What you need	Chairs/boxes and any suitable props for making a train and for having dinner on the train!
How to prepare	Put a few of the boxes or chairs together to simulate a train. Leave other resources near by. This activity is excellent for outsiders and may carry through to several sessions as the play develops.
What to do	Sit down together in a circle and tell the children that you are going on a pretend train journey. You are going to have your dinner on the train, but it's a very funny dinner because it's back to front! Chant these words to sound like a steam train gathering momentum. Churn your arms like the pistons on the wheels. Start very slowly and quietly, getting louder and faster as the chant gathers momentum. *Cof-fee, cof-fee, cof-fee, cof-fee,* *Cheese and biscuits, cheese and biscuits, cheese and biscuits, cheese and biscuits,* *Chocolate pudding, chocolate pudding, chocolate pudding, chocolate pudding,* *Fish and chips, fish and chips, fish and chips, fish and chips,* *SOOOOOOOOOOOOOUP!* As you reach the final line, hold up your arm as if you are sounding the steam whistle. Repeat this a second time now that the children know what to expect. Suggest that you move over to the model train that you have started to build and support the children as they build the rest of it. Try the verse again and make sure someone fetches you dinner! Now stand back as the play develops.
Note	Note examples of the train theme carrying over into their free play.
Things to say	• Can you copy what I do and say what I say? • But we need to be on a train. Where shall we catch one? • Who is going to make us a dinner? What will you use?
Comments	

Creative Development

Area of Learning: Creative Development		
Focus:	**Age Range:**	**Code: CD** _____

Development matters	Play and practical support

Sample activity	
What you need	
How to prepare	
What to do	
Note	
Things to say	
Comments	

Ⓟ

Completed by: **Date:**

Creative Development
(30–60+ months)

Date of activity:	Supervised by:
Children involved:	
Comments	

Date of activity:	Supervised by:
Children involved:	
Comments	

Date of activity:	Supervised by:
Children involved:	
Comments	

Ⓟ

Case study

Case study

A morning in the life of Jack Morris, aged 3 years and 3 months

Time	Activity	Focus
9:00	Jack arrives with his nan and comes straight into the nursery. His nan steadies him and helps to remove his jacket. He hangs it on his peg with the picture of the elephant and puts his flask on the table. His nan draws him back for a quick 'goodbye' but he rushes towards the other children, eager to start the day.	PSED 5 PSED 6
9:05	Jack notices that the computer is free and he sits on the small bench in front of it. He is soon joined by Shani and the two watch the screen for the story of 'Little Red Riding Hood', clicking the mouse to turn the 'pages'. After the story ends, he tells Liz, one of the adults, that he has had his turn now and leaves the bench to join a group of children at the sand tray.	KUW 3 PSED 3
9:15	Jack enjoys a game with Sol, pouring sand over each other's hands. As Sol builds mounds up, Jack smoothes and flattens the sand with his spade. He continues to fill different containers, smoothing them over when they are full, with deep concentration.	PD 3 PSRN 3 KUW 1
9:25	Jack has left the sand tray and has joined a game outside. A pirate area has been created by a group of children who are marching quickly up and down the yard chanting 'we have gold!'. A net has been stretched across one corner and a woven sculpture activity has been adapted into the pirates' hoard as they capture their treasure and poke it through the mesh. Jack finds some paper, screws it up and tries to push it into the mesh, working out how to manage this.	CD 4 PSRN 3
9:35	Jack goes inside to find the trolley. He pulls it outside, carefully negotiating the doorway and the other children, and joins Tamara who is playing with a pile of wooden bricks and planks. They start to fill the trolley with bricks, holding each high and announcing what each 'is' as it tumbles into the trolley – 'A tiger!' he calls. Tamara pulls the trolley as he steadies the load. One of the wooden shapes is a large cone. He tries to fit this into his pocket and finds he has to turn it pointed-end-down in order to poke it in.	PD 1 CD 4 PSRN 3
9:45	The pirates have turned a den into a prison and arranged bins and boards around to enclose their space. There is some negotiation between them about who can come in and who cannot. Jack, one of the younger children in the group, is initially denied. He tries to play with a piece of string but finds that a pirate has the other end of it. After a brief upset, Liz intervenes and helps them to sort out an arrangement together. Jack goes on to collect more string and lengths of wool and, together, the pirates build a web across their door. KUW 2	PSED 3 KUW 2

Time	Activity	Focus
10:00	Jack moves back to the computer where he engages with an early number program. He is joined by an audience of three other children and they all count out loud as each image comes up on the screen. When the computer voice asks, 'What number comes after eight?', the others chant 'Nine!' and Jack watches, listens and echoes. He clicks the mouse appropriately and announces, 'I'm India Jones!'	PSRN 1 KUW 3 PSRN 2
10:05	Jack is attracted back to the pirate area. His friend has come to tell him that the robbers have run away with their money and they need more money to buy candy to give them more power to catch more robbers. Jack comes to help. They have to climb over, under and through various obstacles as they seek for more treasure. They make walkways from low planks balanced onto blocks.	PSED 6 PD 1 KUW 2 PSRN 3
10:10	Jack moves into the making area. He sits and draws, gathering his sheets of paper into a pile ready to take to his nan. He selects many different sizes, colours and shapes of paper and experiments with different coloured pens and crayons.	CD 2
10:15	Snack time is flexible and Jack wanders into the cookery area and selects a baby cucumber which he eyes rather suspiciously, tastes and then abandons. He enjoys a tomato and talks with an adult and a few of his friends as they eat.	PSED 3 CLL 1
10:20	Yesterday, the group had visited a sculpture park and the photographs have already been mounted on card and bound together with treasury tags. Jack sits on the floor with some other children as they look through the photographs and talk about who and what they can see. They recall memories of their trip and talk with their teacher about what they enjoyed most. Their teacher helps them put each photograph into context and think about what each sculpture reminded them of. She helps them develop ideas for their own models and sculptures.	CLL 1 CLL 2 PSED 1 CD 1
10:25	The same photographs and more have been loaded into the computer and the children continue to enjoy watching and talking about pictures of their visit. As they crane to see the images, Liz suggests that Jack needs to sit down as his feet are going into Sam's space. He sits where they can all see, leaping up whenever he catches sight of himself or his nan. One picture is of Jack on a miniature train looking brave and this gives the teacher the opportunity to talk about feelings.	PD 2 PSED 2 PSED 4

A morning in the life of Jack Morris, aged 3 years and 3 months continued

Time	Activity	Focus
10:35	Jack moves to a writing area and wipes the whiteboard clean. He grasps the pens with a fisted grasp and enjoys making large circular movements and mark-making within the enclosed spaces that he has created.	CLL 6
10:40	Jack is at a table of dough. He selects a cutter and makes indentations into his ball of dough. He searches for other resources and begins to cut and mould shapes to fit a patty-pan tray. He works out that he needs to flatten his balls of dough in order to make impressions with the cutters.	KUW 2 PD 3 PSRN 3
10:45	Jack is helped to put his jacket on and he moves outside into the larger of two yards to play. He hangs and swings from the climbing frame. He spots that a tricycle has become available and makes a dash for it. There is a brief skirmish as Jack and another child negotiate whose turn it is and one of the older children steps in to help. Jack then briefly becomes one of many goal keepers in a game of football. Another skirmish results in Jack accidentally pushing over another child who falls and hurts his nose. Liz steps in to help and Jack's teacher talks to him about what has happened. Jack goes indoors to sit quietly with her for a while.	PSED 5 PD 1 PSED 4 PSED 3 PD 3 PSED 4 PSED 3
10:55	Jack is intrigued by a model helicopter and examines it carefully, turning its blades with his fingers and opening the doors. He moves on to the construction area and begins to make his own miniature sculpture – it looks like a cross between a helicopter and a flying bug, based on some of the sculptures that he had seen yesterday. He adds more pipe cleaners and then concludes, 'My's a e'fant!' ('Mine's an elephant!').	KUW 1 CD 1 CD 2
11:05	It is tidy-up time. Jack joins in a little with encouragement and is thanked for helping.	PSED 6
11:15	Jack helps his teacher choose the story. They choose his favourite and he sits quietly in the group, enthralled by the story and the pictures. Sometimes he joins in with the familiar catchphrases as the teacher pauses for the children to join in. For a little while, he is distracted by a board game on a nearby shelf, but soon leaves this to follow the story again.	CLL 4
11:25	The parents and carers have arrived. He remembers his pictures and collects them to show proudly to his nan who is waiting outside the door. She helps him with his coat, reminds him to fetch his flask and he is off home.	PSED 2

References

DCFS (2007 & revised 2008) *The Early Years Foundation Stage*. Nottingham: DCFS Publications.

Gallow, C. (2007) *Trackers 0-5: Tracking Children's Progress through the Early Years Foundation Stage*. Stafford: QEd Publications.

Mortimer, H. (2000) *Playladders*. Stafford: QEd Publications.

Mortimer, H. (2001) *The Observation and Assessment of Children in the Early Years*. Stafford: QEd Publications.

Mortimer, H. (2008) *Music Makers: Music circle times to include everyone*. Stafford: QEd Publications.

Rowlands, H. & Mortimer, H. (2008) *Making the Early Years Foundation Stage work for you (0-36 months)*. Stafford: QEd Publications.

Area of Learning:		
Focus:	Age Range:	Code: _____
Development matters		Play and practical support

Sample activity	
What you need	
How to prepare	
What to do	
Note	
Things to say	
Comments	

Ⓟ

Completed by: **Date:**

Area of Learning:		
Focus:	Age Range:	Code: _____
Development matters	Play and practical support	

Sample activity	
What you need	
How to prepare	
What to do	
Note	
Things to say	
Comments	

Ⓟ

Completed by: **Date:**